FIRST 50 TV THEMES

YOU SHOULD PLAY ON THE PIANO

ISBN 978-1-5400-5307-7

Visit Hal Leonard Online at
www.halleonard.com

Contact us:
Hal Leonard
7777 West Bluemound Road
Milwaukee, WI 53213
Email: info@halleonard.com

In Europe, contact:
Hal Leonard Europe Limited
42 Wigmore Street
Marylebone, London, W1U 2RN
Email: info@halleonardeurope.com

In Australia, contact:
Hal Leonard Australia Pty. Ltd.
4 Lentara Court
Cheltenham, Victoria, 3192 Australia
Email: info@halleonard.com.au

THE AMERICANS MAIN TITLE

from the Twentieth Century Fox Television Series THE AMERICANS

Music by NATHAN BARR

ADDAMS FAMILY THEME
Theme from the TV Show and Movie

Music and Lyrics by
VIC MIZZY

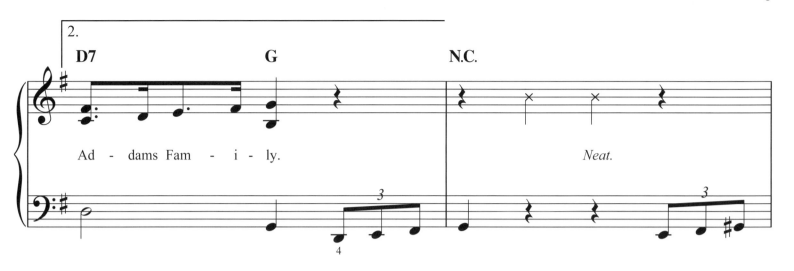

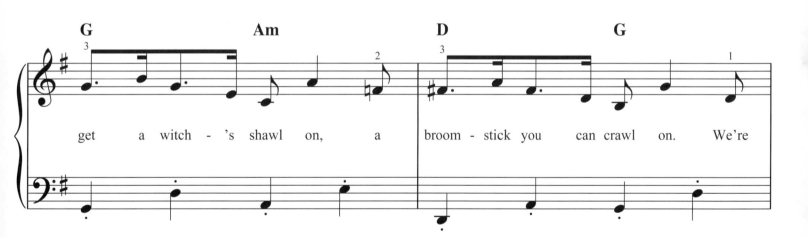

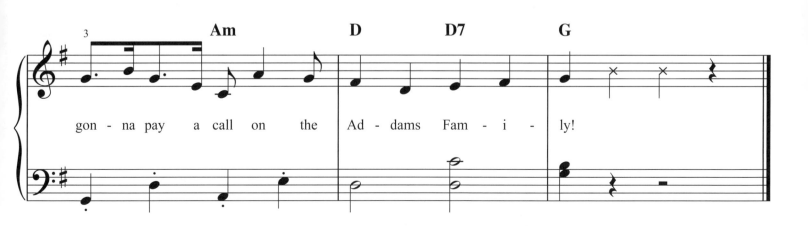

BEMIDJI, MN
from the TV Series FARGO

Music by JEFF RUSSO

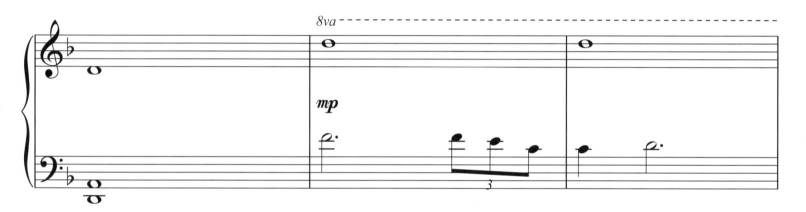

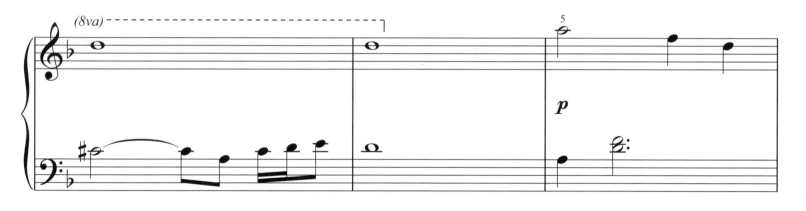

BROOKLYN NINE-NINE
(Theme)

Words and Music by
DANIEL BRENDAN MAROCCO

Quickly

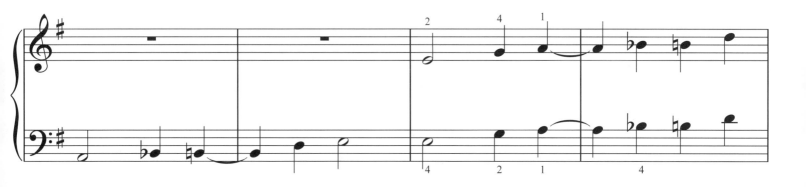

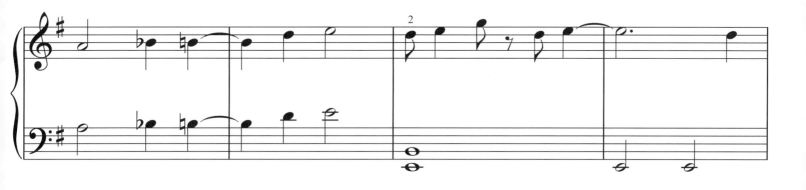

THE BIG BANG THEORY

Words and Music by
ED ROBERTSON

Moderately fast

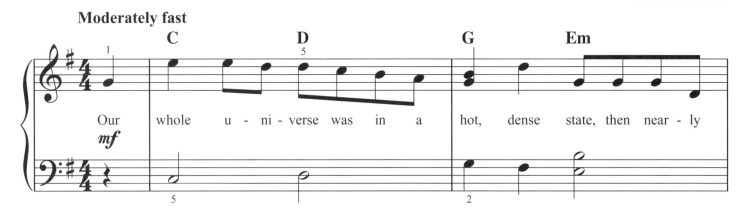

Our whole u - ni - verse was in a hot, dense state, then near - ly

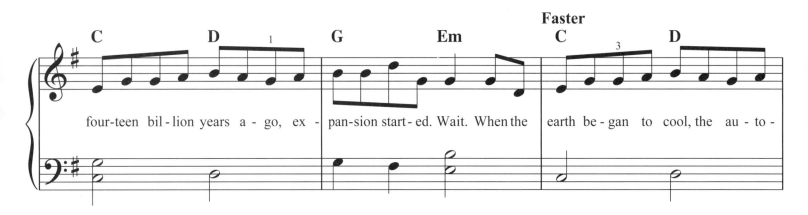

four-teen bil - lion years a - go, ex - pan-sion start - ed. Wait. When the earth be - gan to cool, the au - to -

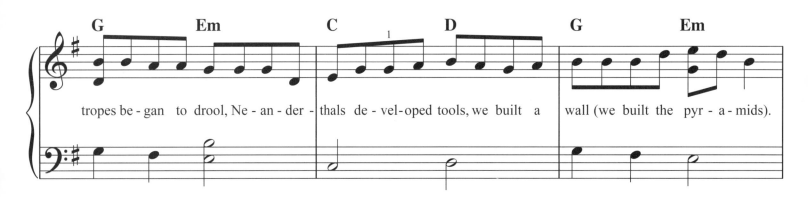

tropes be - gan to drool, Ne - an - der - thals de - vel -oped tools, we built a wall (we built the pyr - a - mids).

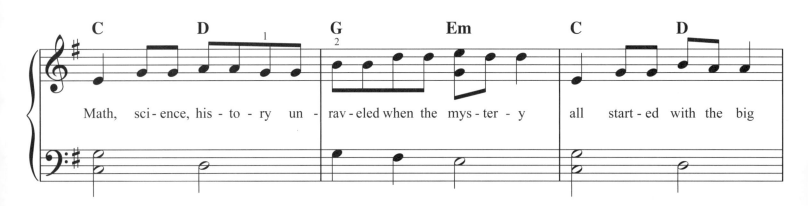

Math, sci - ence, his - to - ry un - rav -eled when the mys - ter - y all start - ed with the big

bang. (Bang!) Since the dawn of man it's real-ly not that long, as ev-'ry

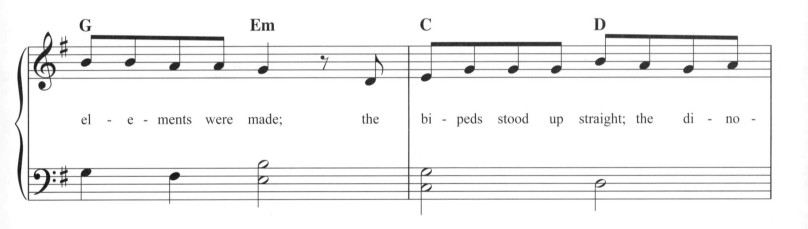

gal-ax-y was born in less time than it takes to sing this song. A frac-tion of a sec-ond,then the

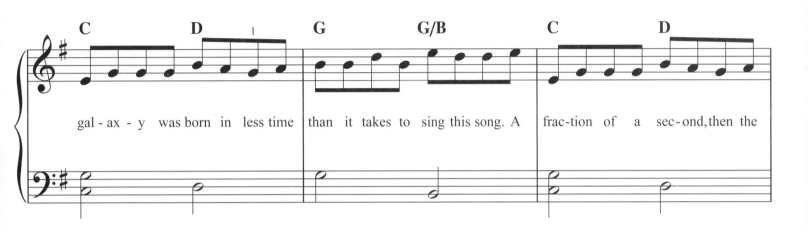

el-e-ments were made; the bi-peds stood up straight; the di-no-

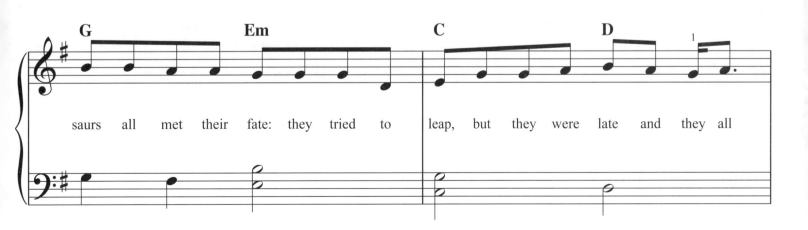

saurs all met their fate: they tried to leap, but they were late and they all

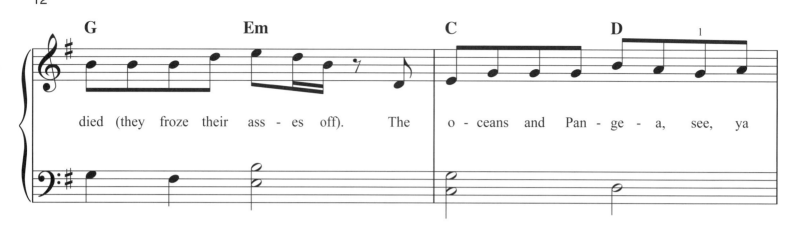

died (they froze their ass - es off). The o - ceans and Pan - ge - a, see, ya

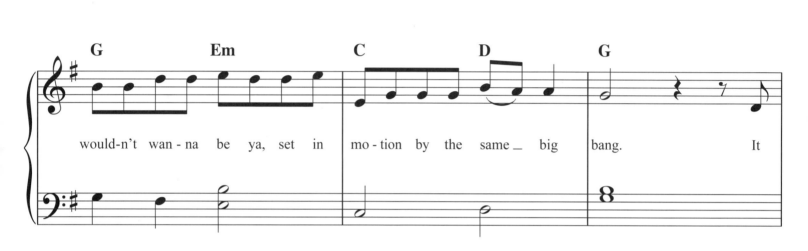

would-n't wan - na be ya, set in mo - tion by the same big bang. It

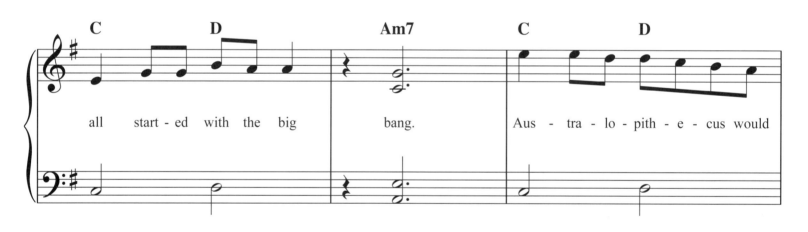

all start - ed with the big bang. Aus - tra - lo - pith - e - cus would

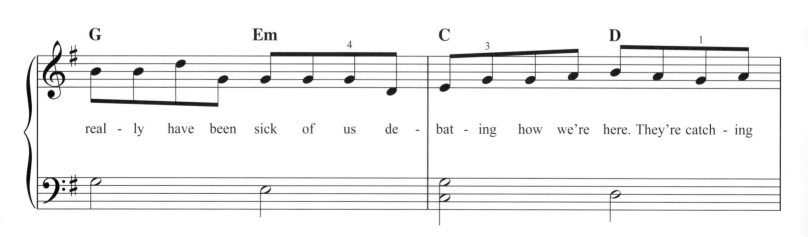

real - ly have been sick of us de - bat - ing how we're here. They're catch - ing

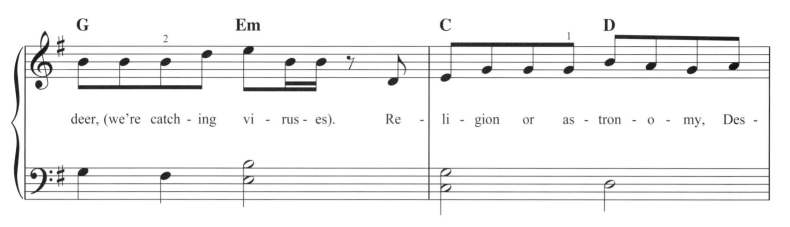

deer, (we're catch - ing vi - rus - es). Re - li - gion or as - tron - o - my, Des -

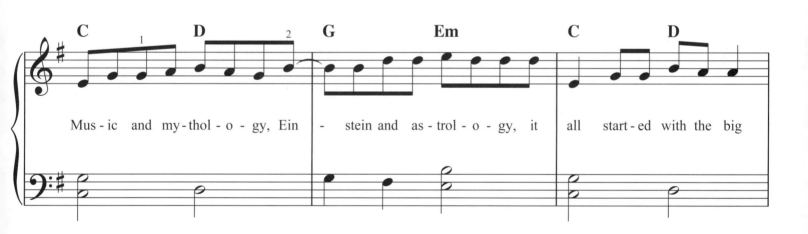

cartes or Deu - ter - on - o - my, it all start - ed with the big bang.

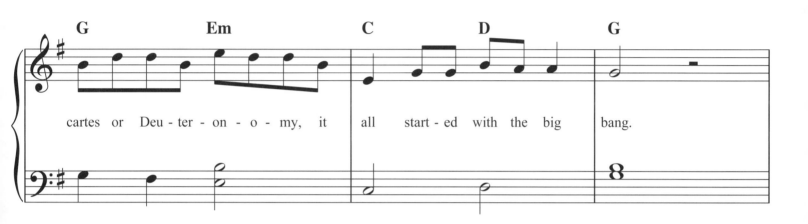

Mus - ic and my - thol - o - gy, Ein - stein and as - trol - o - gy, it all start - ed with the big

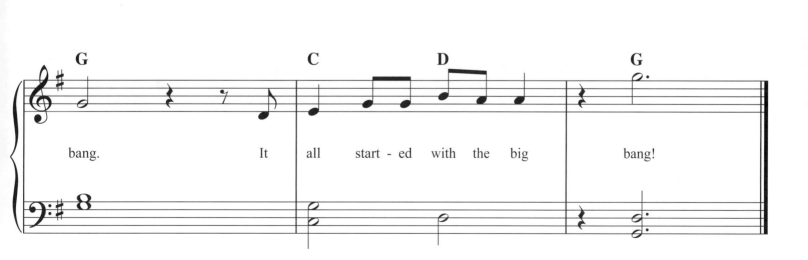

bang. It all start - ed with the big bang!

THE BRADY BUNCH
Theme from the Paramount Television Series THE BRADY BUNCH

Words and Music by SHERWOOD SCHWARTZ
and FRANK DEVOL

Moderately fast, in 2

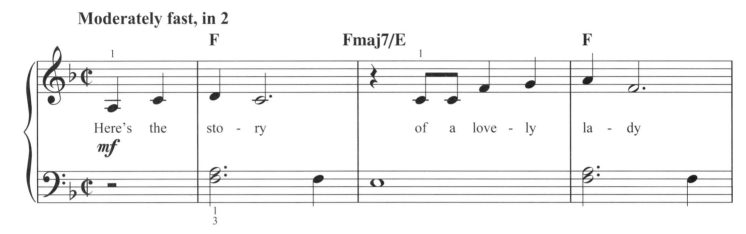

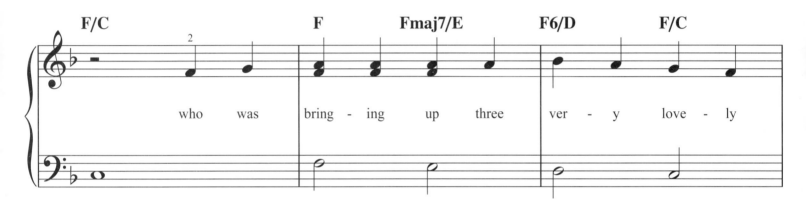

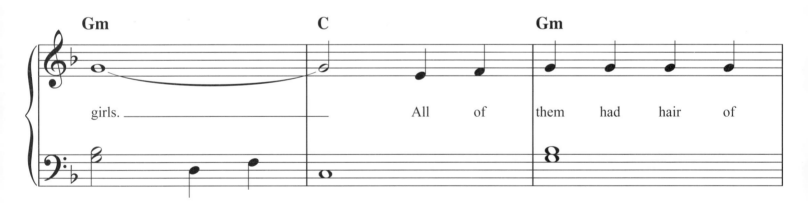

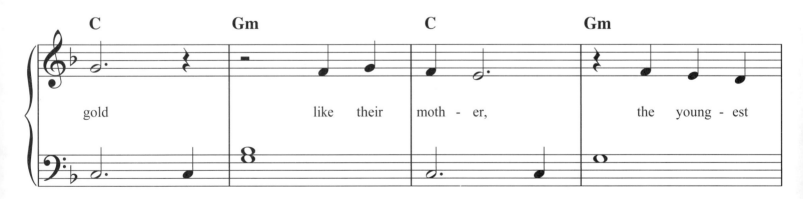

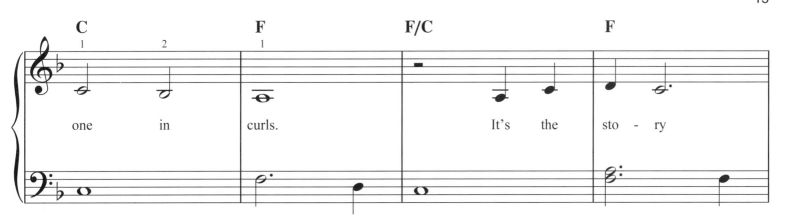

one   in   curls.   It's the sto - ry

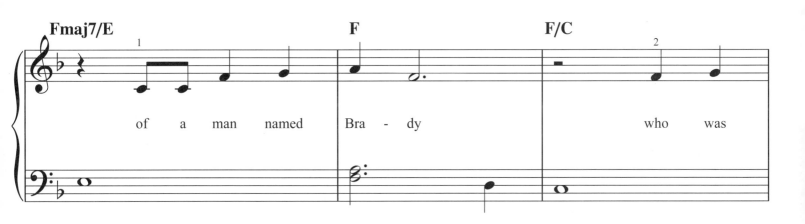

of a man named Bra - dy who was

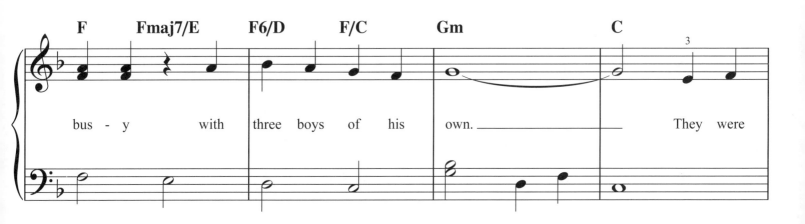

bus - y with three boys of his own. They were

four men liv - ing all to - geth - er,

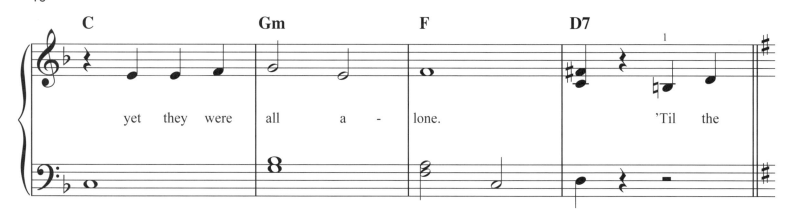

C   **Gm**   **F**   **D7**

yet they were all a - lone. 'Til the

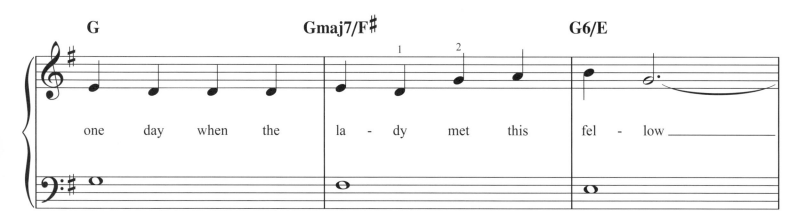

G   **Gmaj7/F♯**   **G6/E**

one day when the la - dy met this fel - low _____

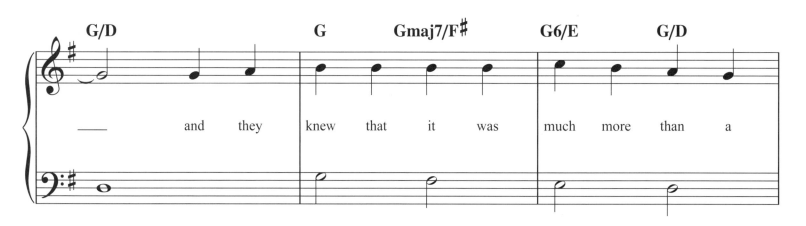

G/D   **G**   **Gmaj7/F♯**   **G6/E**   **G/D**

_____ and they knew that it was much more than a

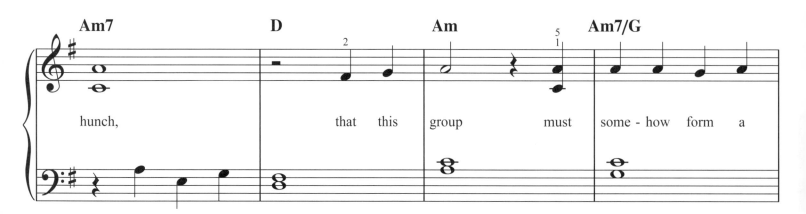

Am7   **D**   **Am**   **Am7/G**

hunch, that this group must some - how form a

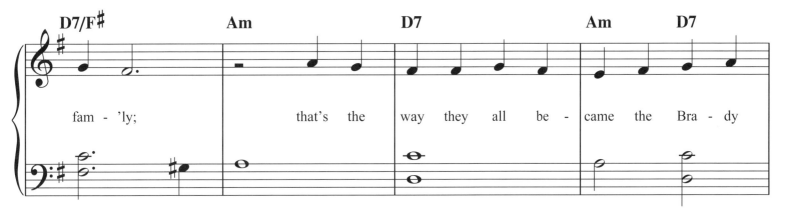

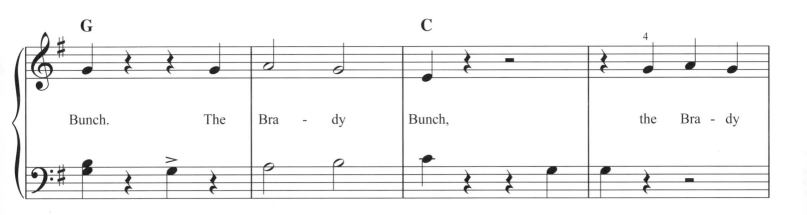

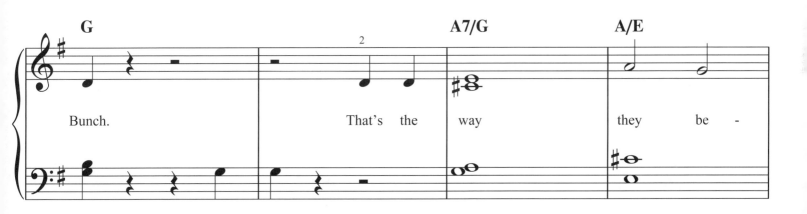

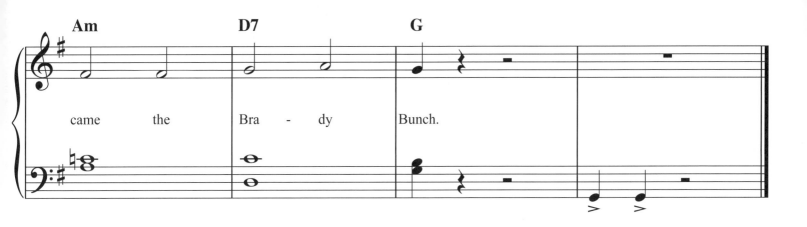

CBS SPORTS NFL THEME

By ELLIOT SCHRAEGER
and WALTER LEVINSKY

D.S. al Coda

CODA

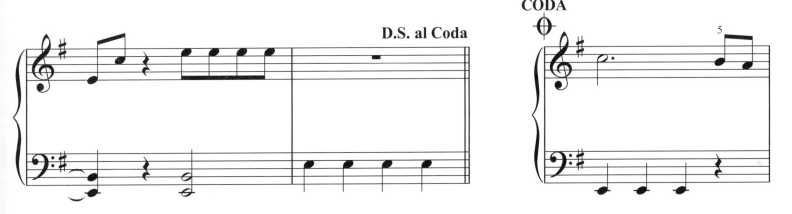

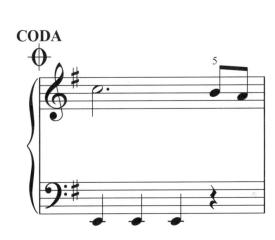

CHANGING KEYS
(Wheel of Fortune Theme)

Music by MERV GRIFFIN

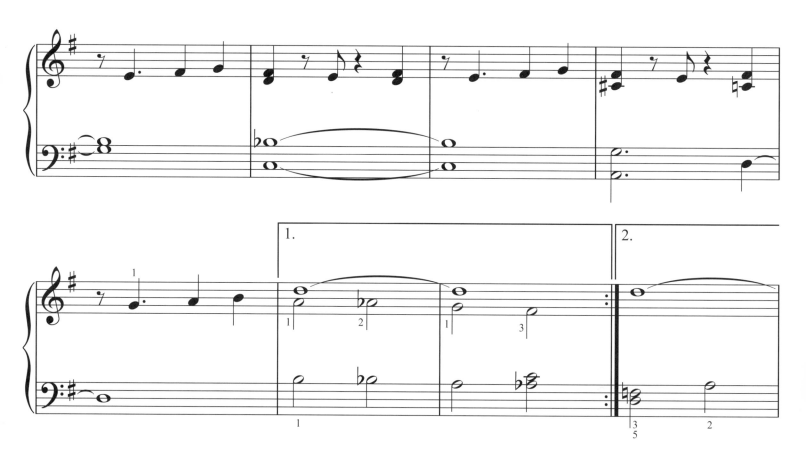

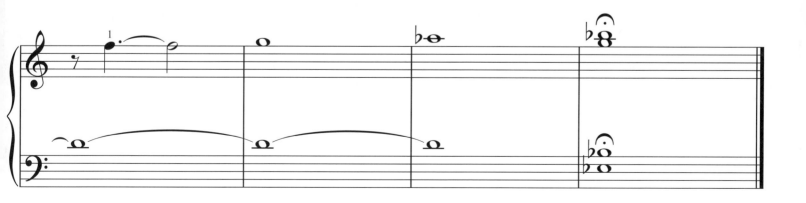

DR. WHO XI

By MURRAY GOLD

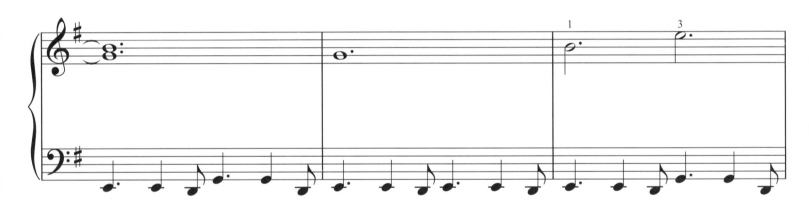

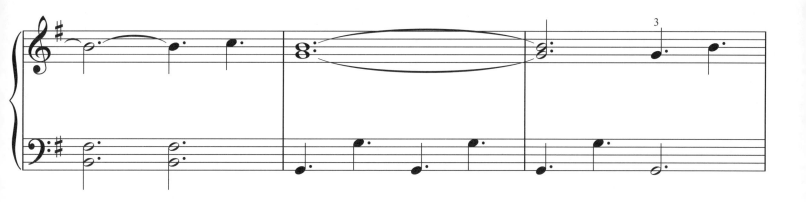

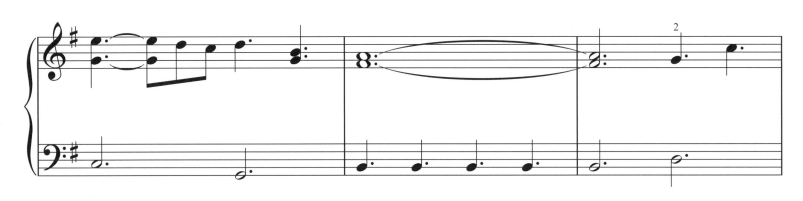

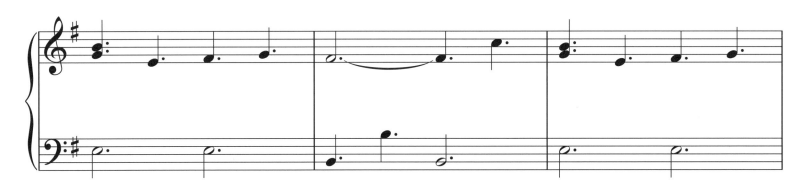

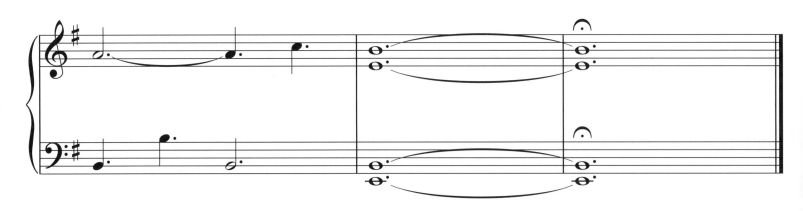

EVERYWHERE YOU LOOK
(Theme from FULL HOUSE)

Words and Music by JEFFREY FRANKLIN,
JESSE FREDERICK and BENNETT SALVAY

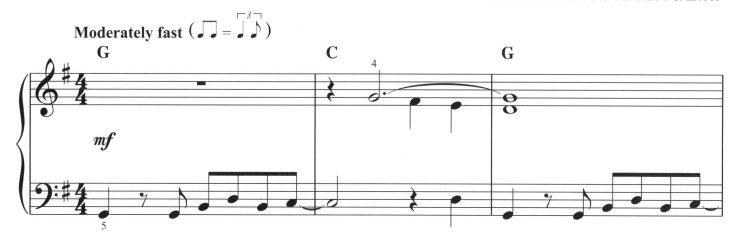

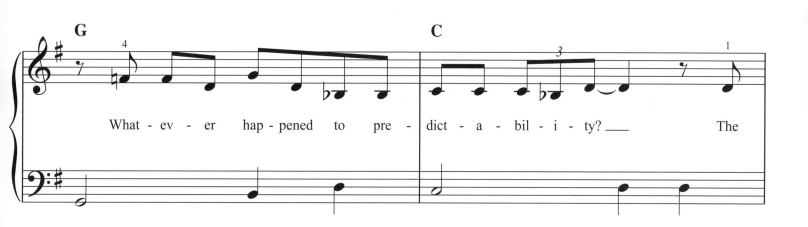

What - ev - er hap - pened to pre - dict - a - bil - i - ty? ___ The

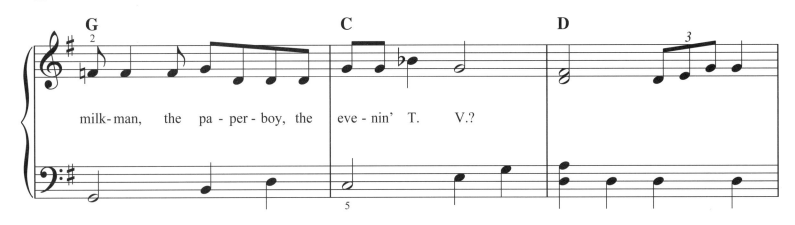

milk-man, the pa-per-boy, the eve-nin' T. V.?

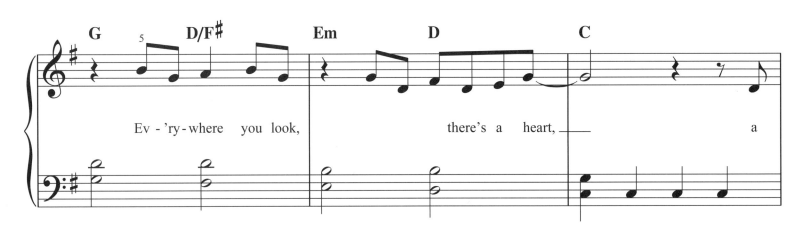

Ev-'ry-where you look, there's a heart, _____ a

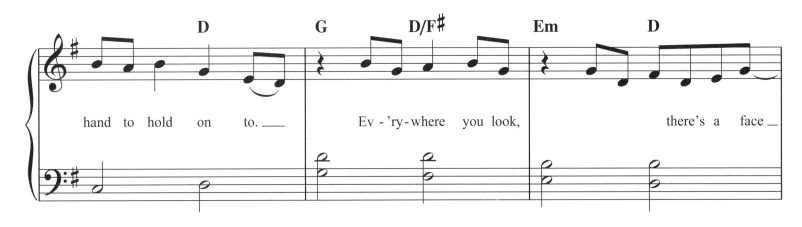

hand to hold on to. ___ Ev-'ry-where you look, there's a face _

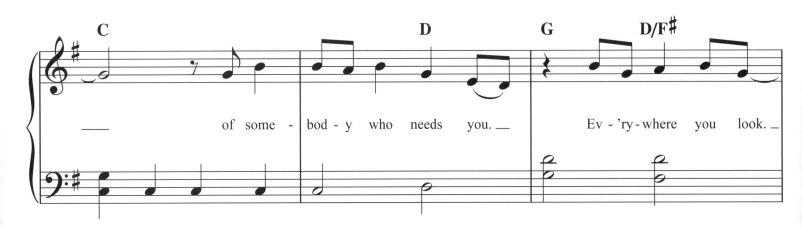

___ of some-bod-y who needs you. ___ Ev-'ry-where you look. _

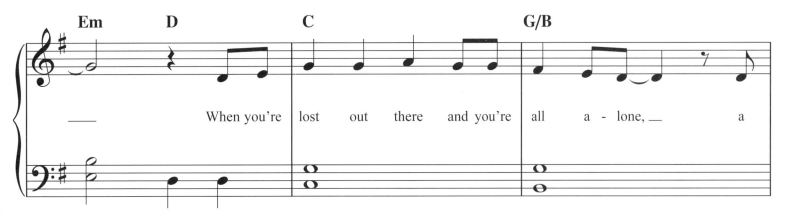

Em   D   C   G/B

When you're lost out there and you're all a - lone, ___ a

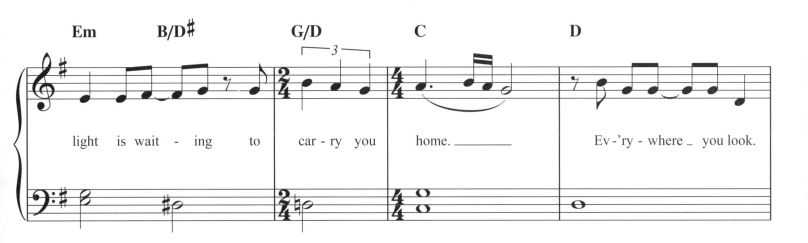

Em   B/D♯   G/D   C   D

light is wait - ing to car - ry you home. ___ Ev -'ry - where _ you look.

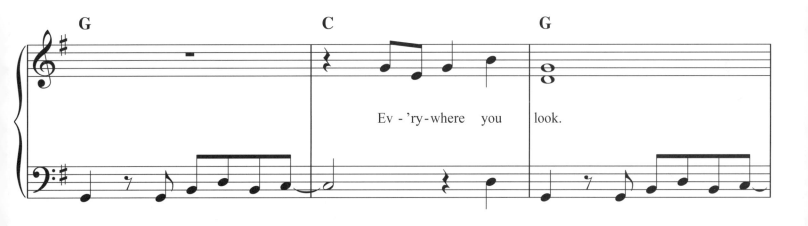

G   C   G

Ev -'ry-where you look.

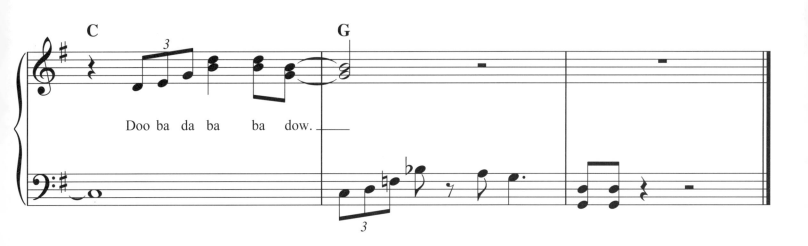

C   G

Doo ba da ba ba dow. ___

DOWNTON ABBEY
(Theme)

Music by JOHN LUNN

Moving along

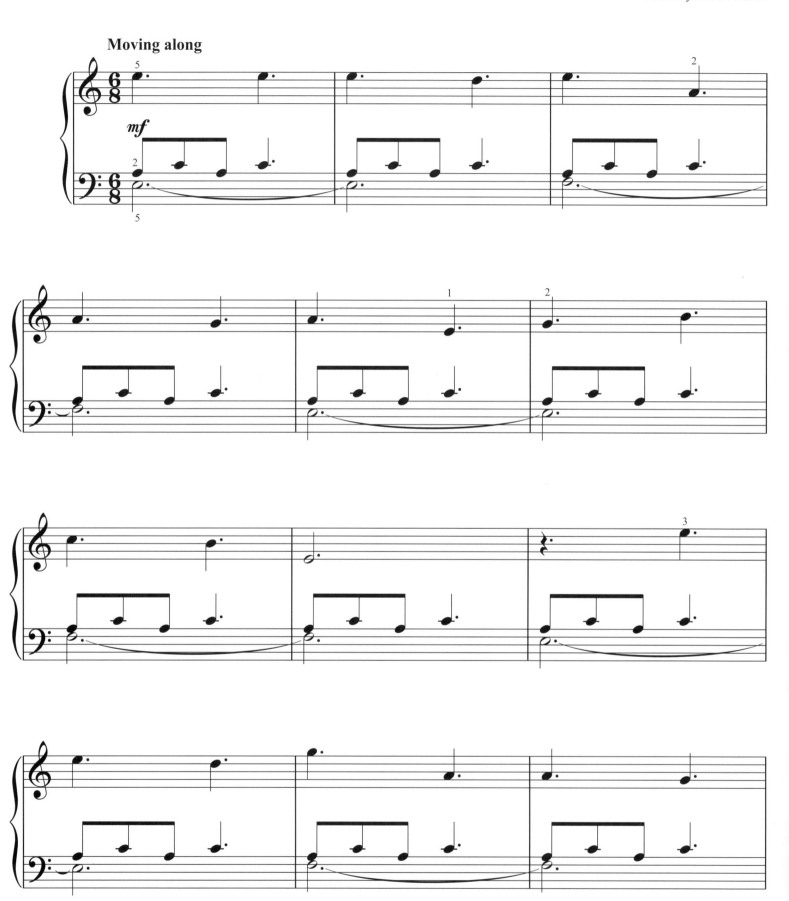

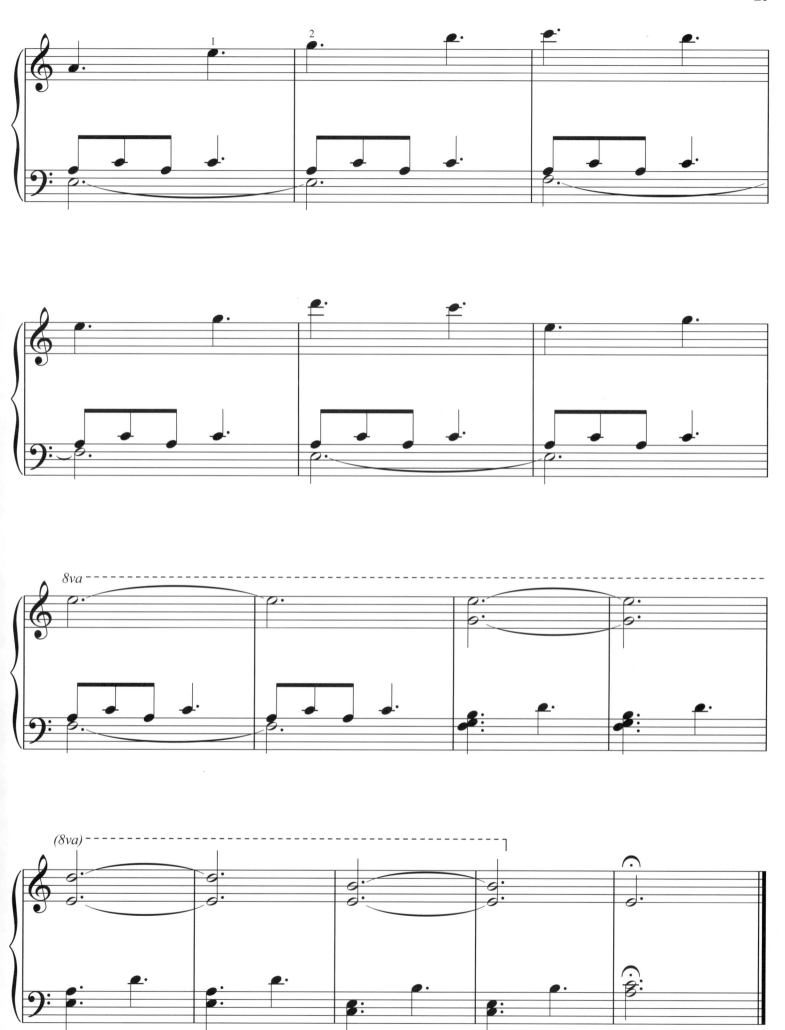

E.R.
(Main Theme)

By JAMES NEWTON HOWARD

EVERYBODY LOVES RAYMOND
(Opening Theme)

Words and Music by TERRY TROTTER
and RICK MAROTTA

THEME FROM FAMILY GUY

from the Twentieth Century Fox Television Series FAMILY GUY

Words by SETH MacFARLANE
and DAVID ZUCKERMAN
Music by WALTER MURPHY

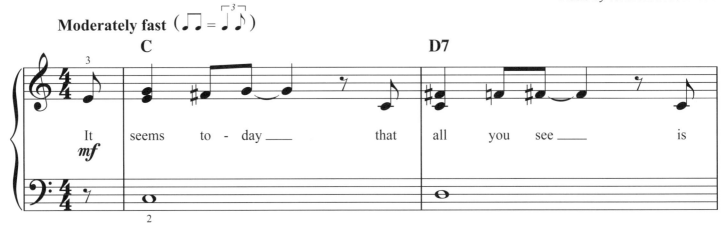

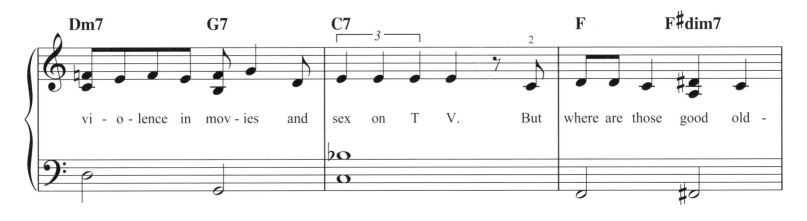

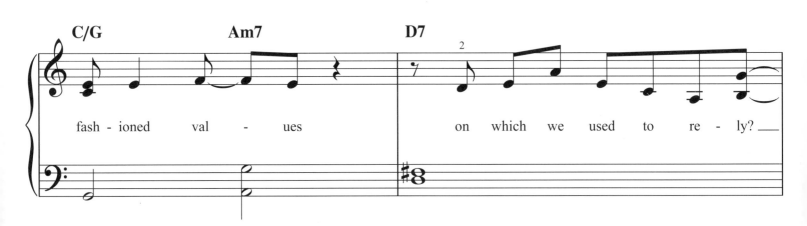

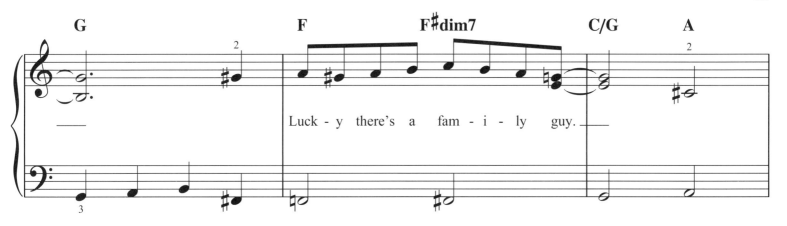

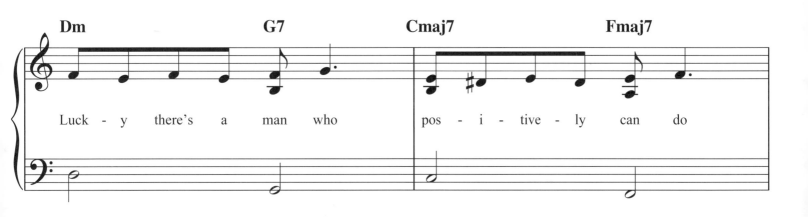

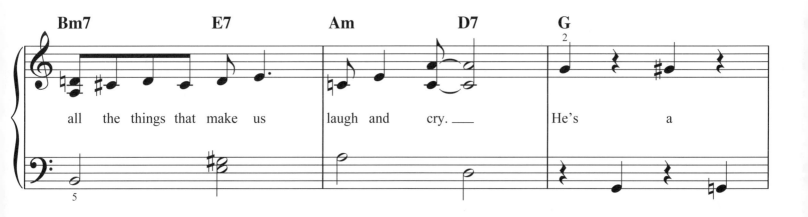

FRASIER – END TITLE
(Theme from Fraiser)
from the TV Series FRASIER

Words by DARRYL PHINNESSEE
and BRUCE MILLER
Music by BRUCE MILLER

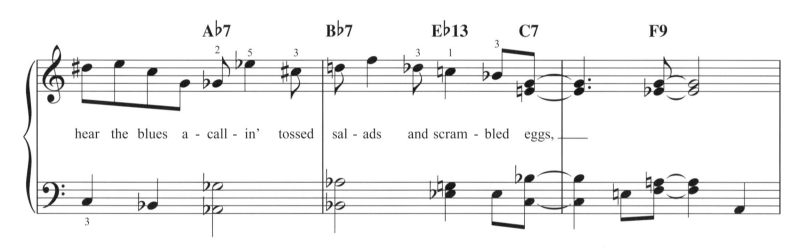

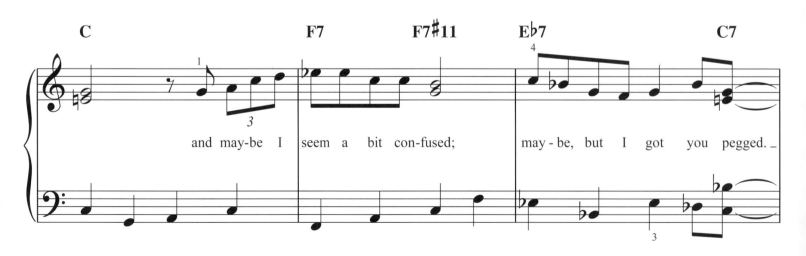

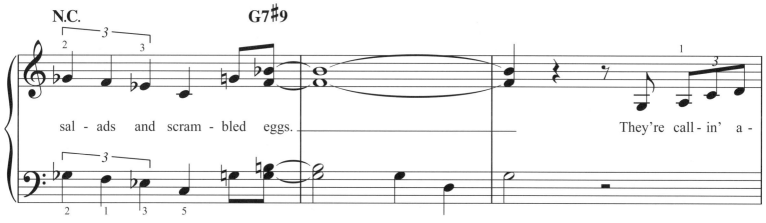

GAME OF THRONES
Theme from the HBO Series GAME OF THRONES

By RAMIN DJAWADI

Moderately fast (in 1)

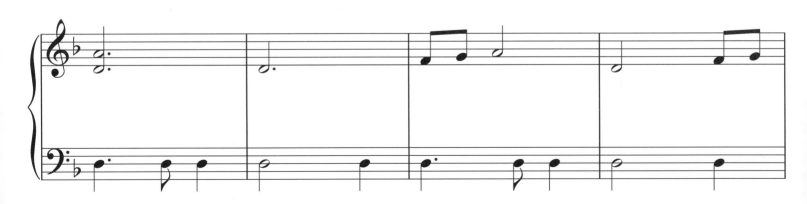

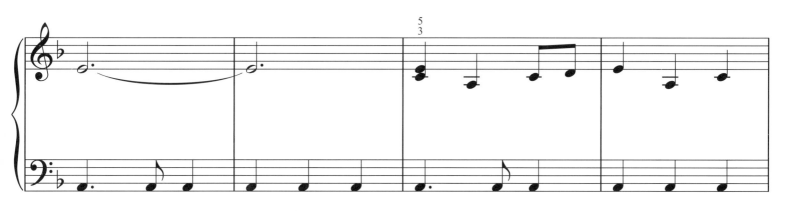

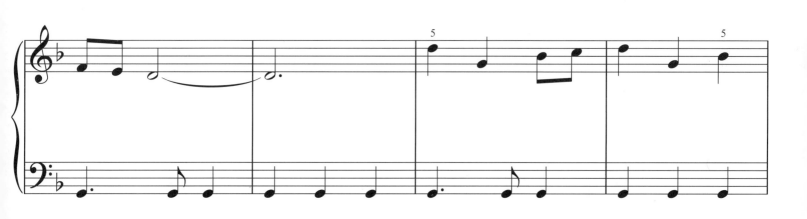

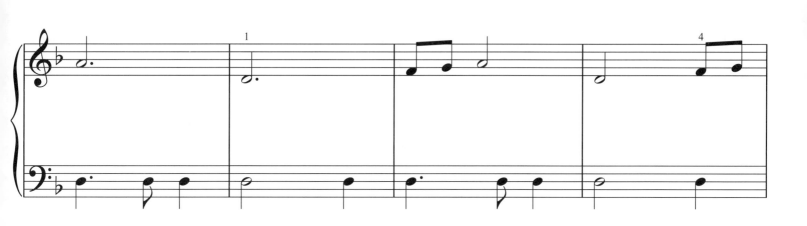

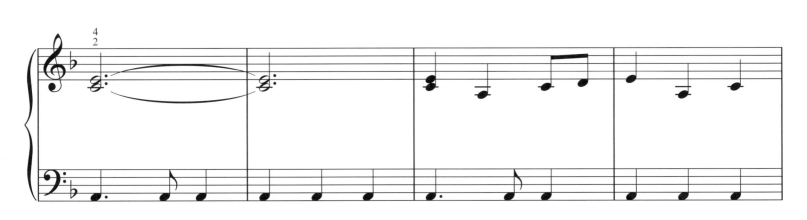

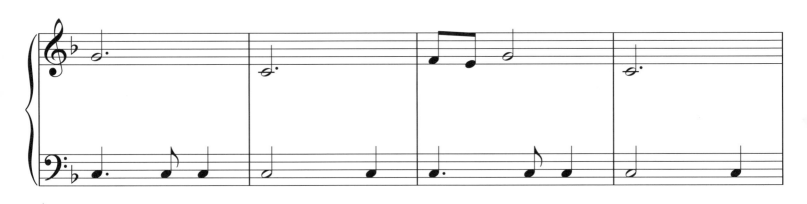

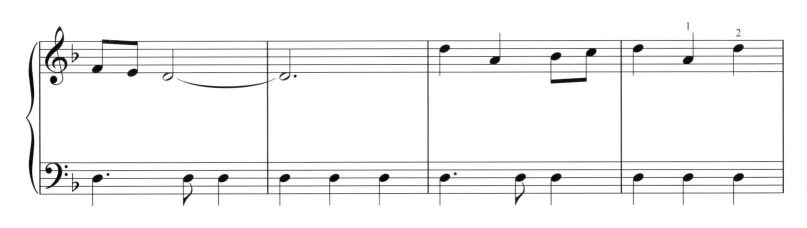

THE GOLDBERGS MAIN TITLE

Music by BRIAN MAZZAFERRI

To Coda ⊕

But I would-n't change a thing, 'cause all ___ those things were

mine. So we'll re - wind.

There's a Po - lar - oid pic - ture in my

mind: it's me at twelve years old. And I ___ wan - na tell that kid that he's al -

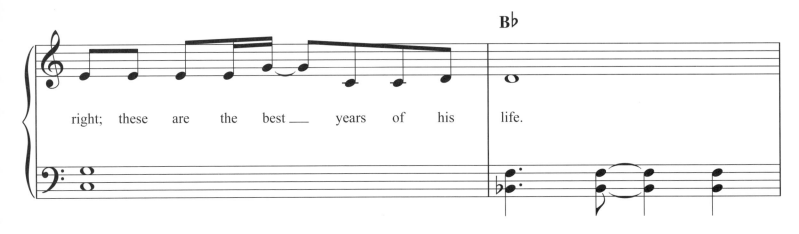

right; these are the best ___ years of his life.

G **C**

There's an eight - bit game in - side my

head. Just one more hit, and I'll be dead. ___ I duck and jump and charge a -

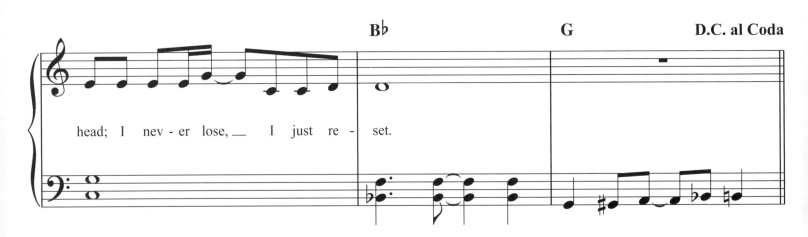

head; I nev - er lose, ___ I just re - set.

CODA

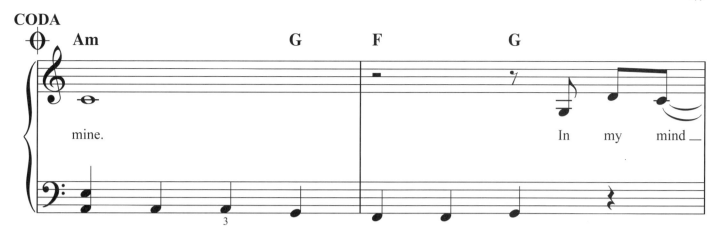

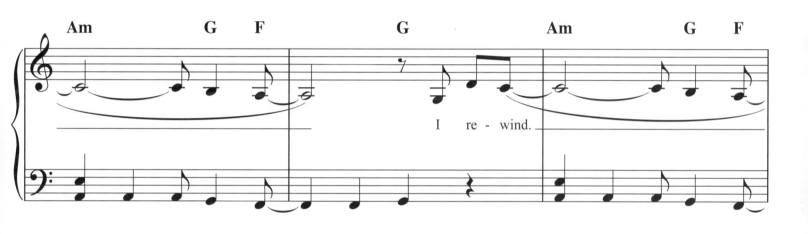

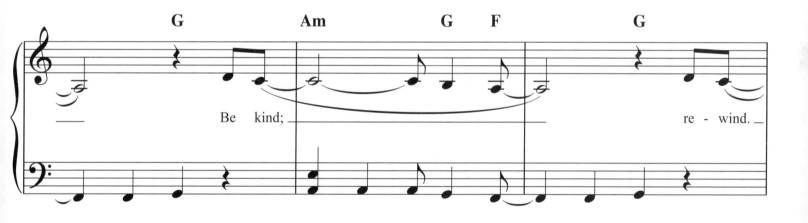

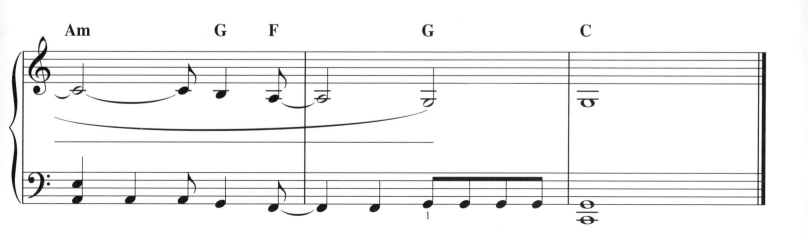

HAPPY DAYS
Theme from the Paramount Television Series HAPPY DAYS

Words by NORMAN GIMBEL
Music by CHARLES FOX

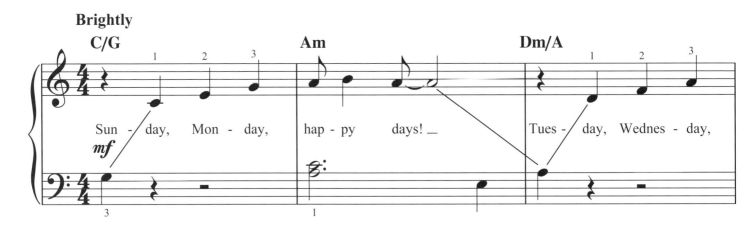

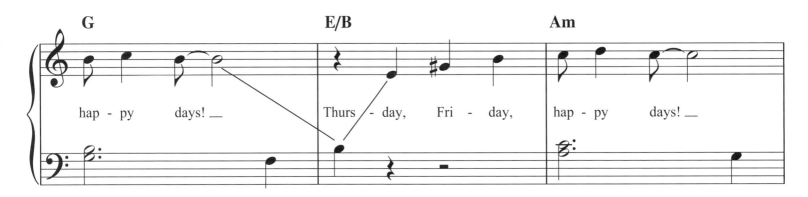

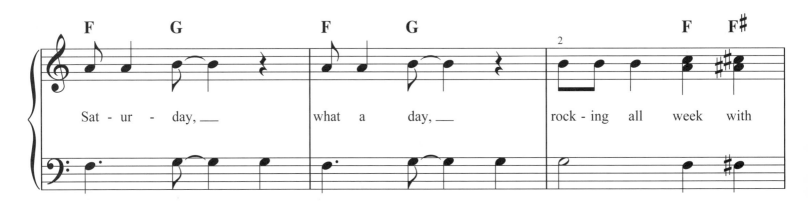

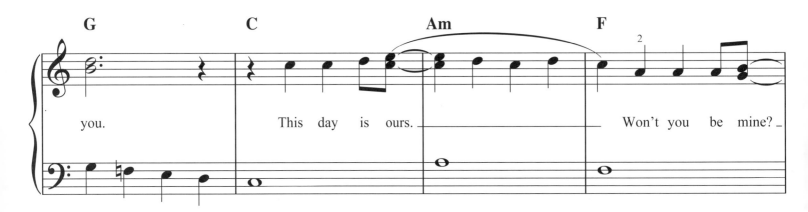

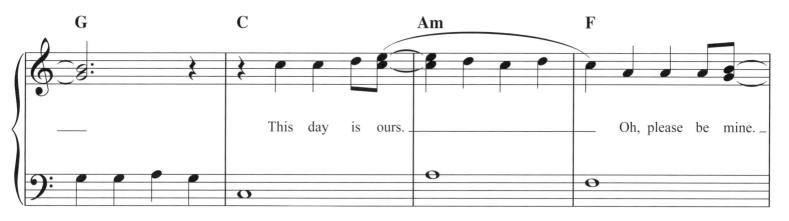

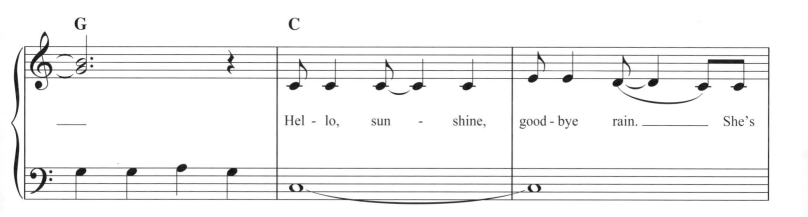

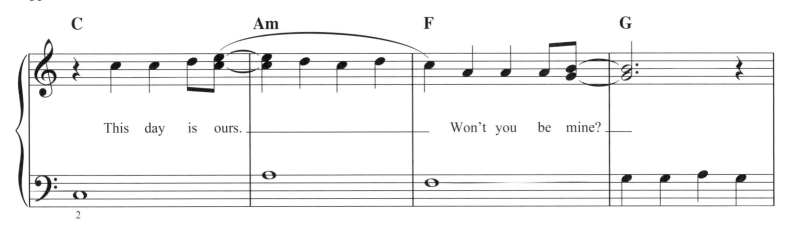

This day is ours. _____ Won't you be mine? ___

This day is ours. _____ Oh, please be mine. ___

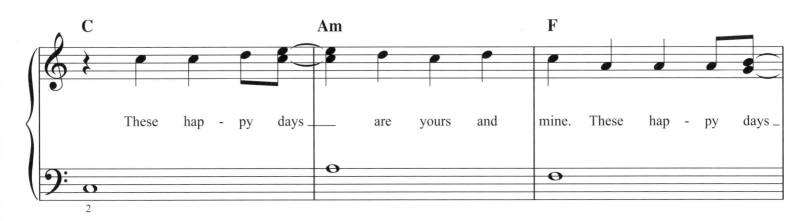

These hap - py days ___ are yours and mine. These hap - py days ___

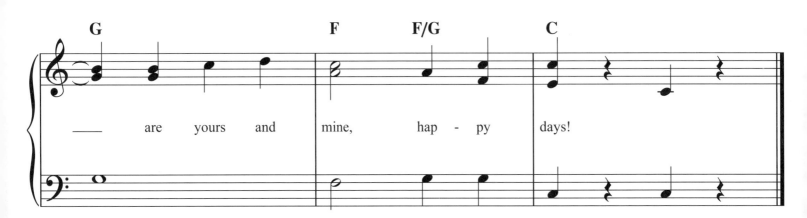

___ are yours and mine, hap - py days!

HEY BEAUTIFUL
from HOW I MET YOUR MOTHER

Words and Music by CARTER BAYS
and CRAIG THOMAS

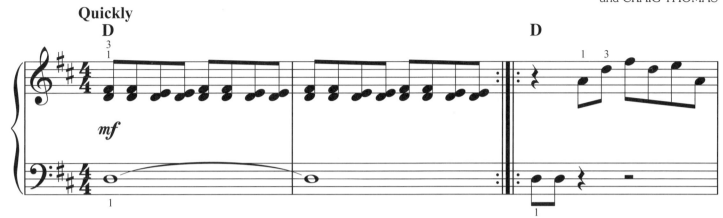

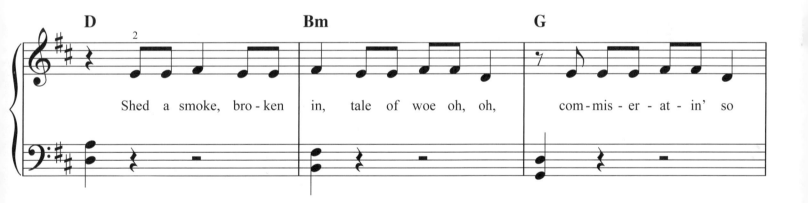

Shed a smoke, bro-ken in, tale of woe oh, oh, com-mis-er-at-in' so

hard to let go. I'm on your back, scratch-in' ear-ly and your can-di-date,

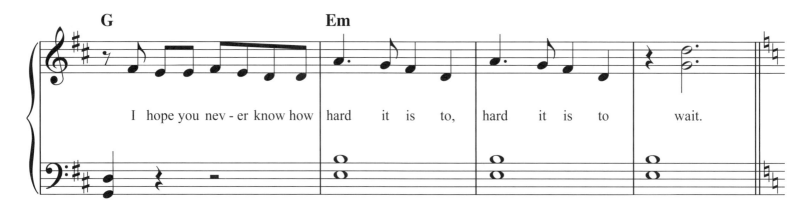

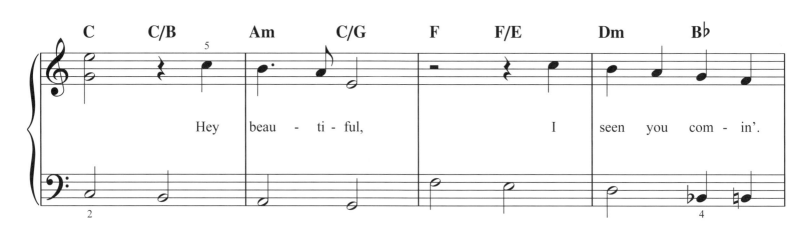

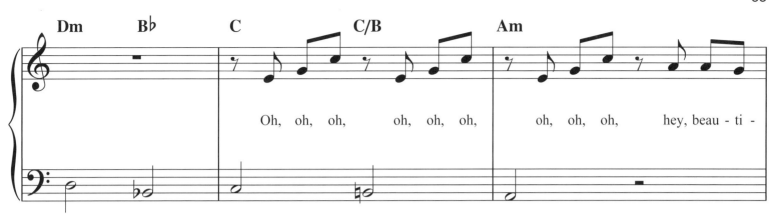

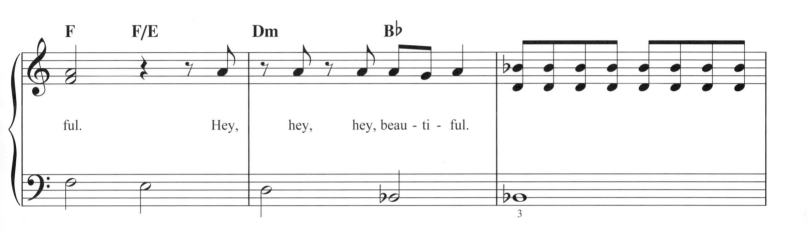

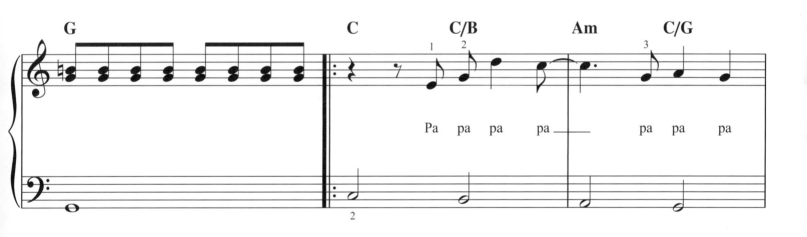

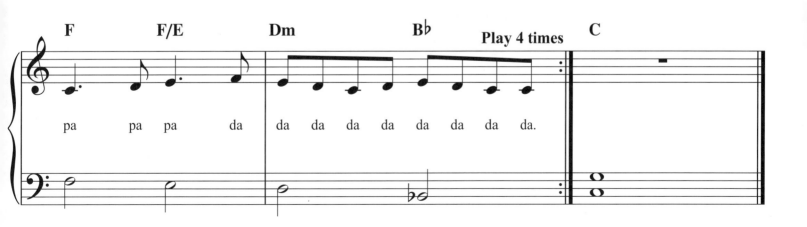

HAWAII FIVE-O THEME

from the Television Series

By MORT STEVENS

With a driving beat

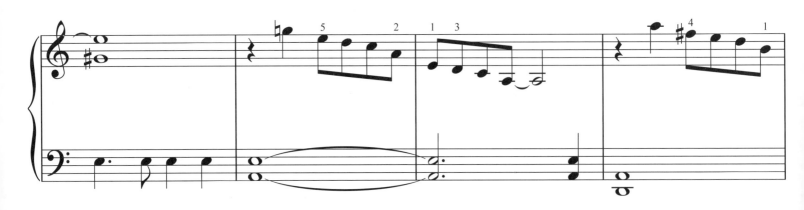

I LOVE LUCY

from the Television Series

Lyric by HAROLD ADAMSON
Music by ELIOT DANIEL

Moderately

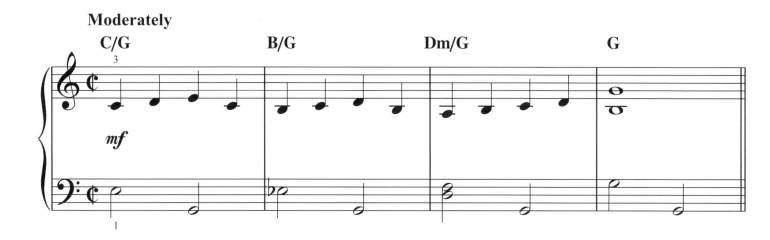

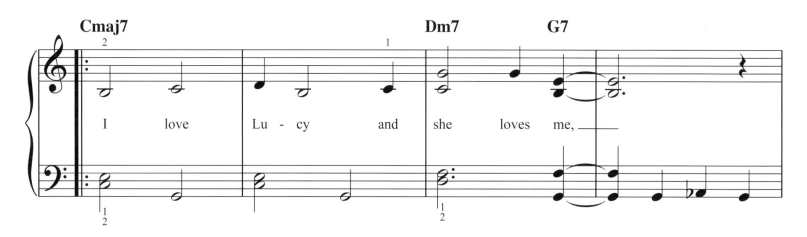

I love Lu - cy and she loves me,

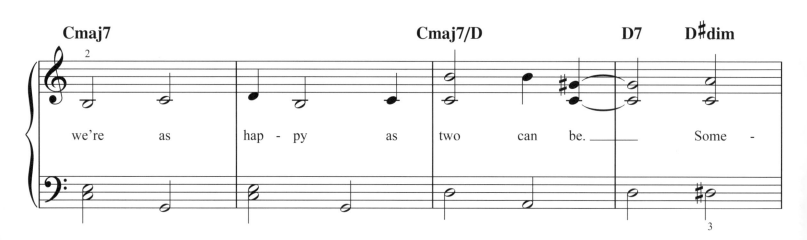

we're as hap - py as two can be. Some -

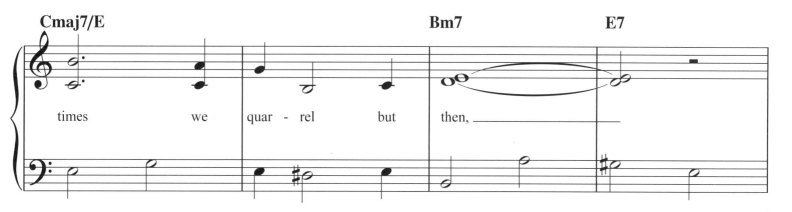

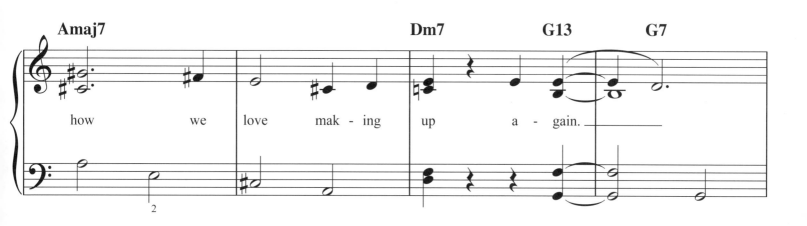

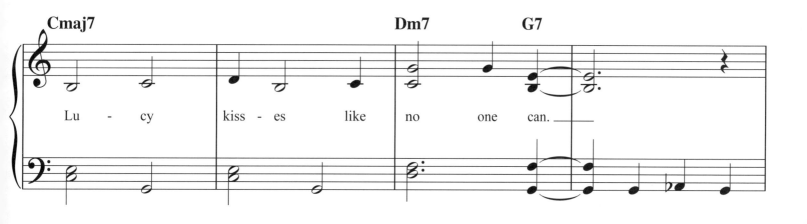

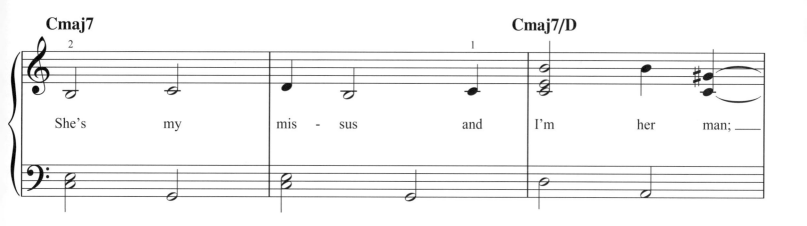

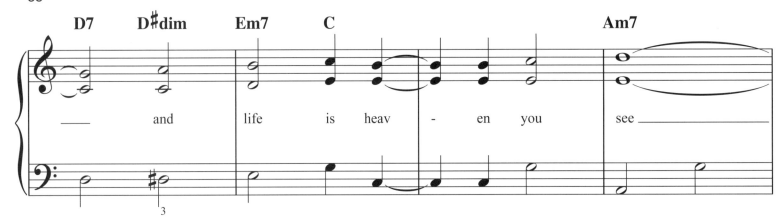

and life is heav - en you see ____

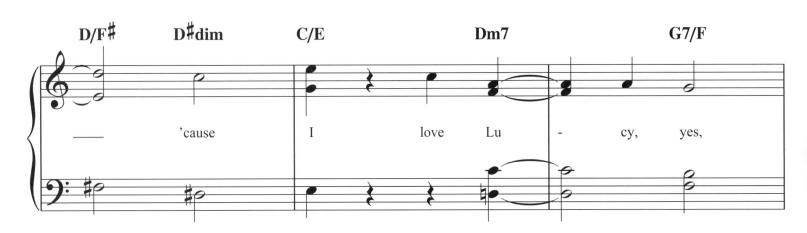

____ 'cause I love Lu - cy, yes,

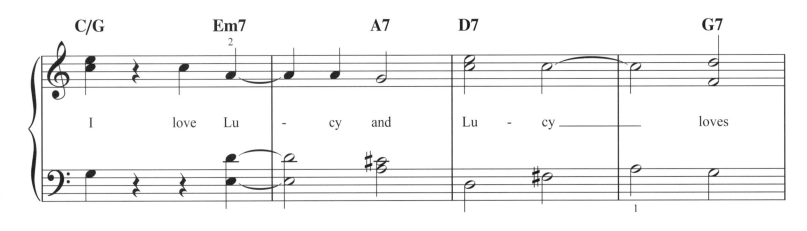

I love Lu - cy and Lu - cy ____ loves

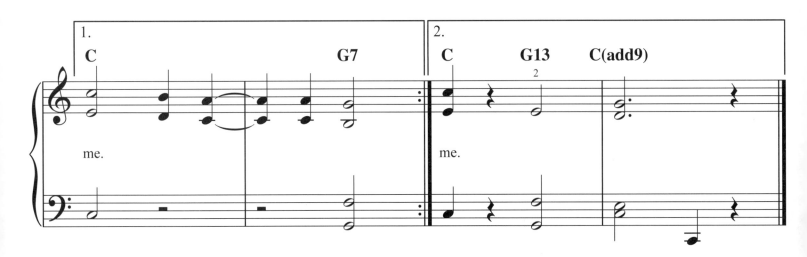

me. | me.

I'LL BE THERE FOR YOU
(Theme from "Friends")

Words by DAVID CRANE,
MARTA KAUFFMAN, ALLEE WILLIS,
PHIL SOLEM and DANNY WILDE
Music by MICHAEL SKLOFF

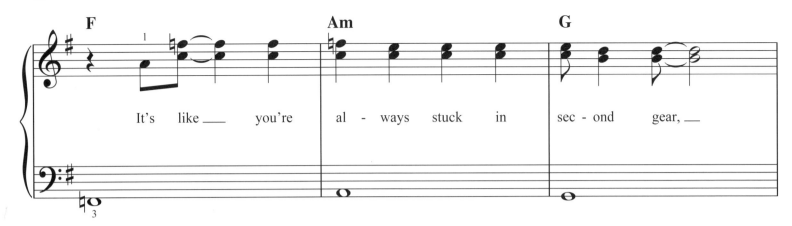

It's like ___ you're al - ways stuck in sec - ond gear, ___

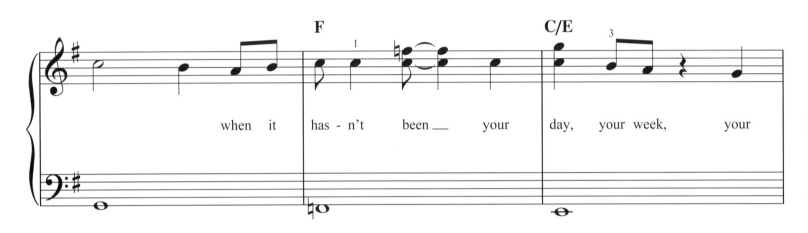

when it has - n't been ___ your day, your week, your

month, or e - ven your year. But I'll ___ be

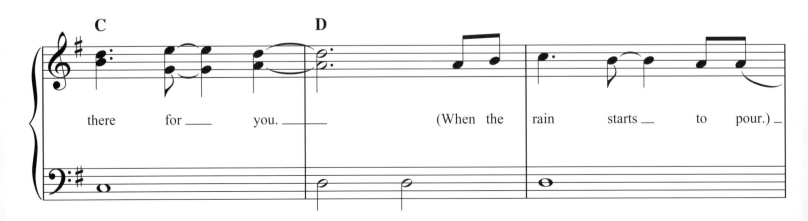

there for ___ you. ___ (When the rain starts ___ to pour.) ___

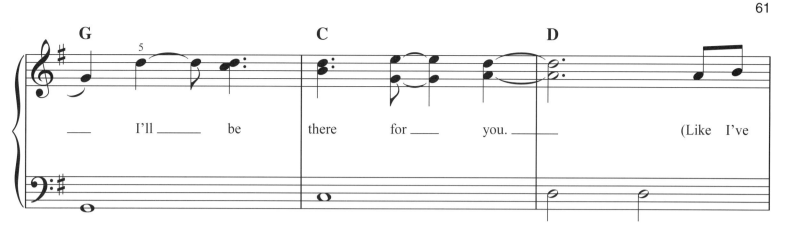

I'll ___ be   there   for ___   you. ___   (Like I've

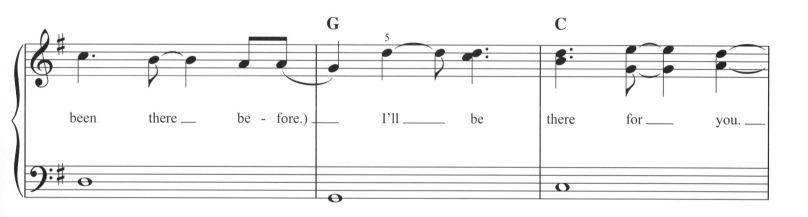

been   there ___   be - fore.) ___   I'll ___   be   there   for ___   you. ___

___   'cause you're   there   for ___   me   too. ___

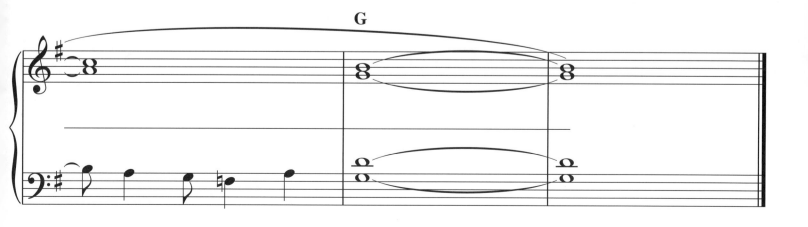

IT'S A JUNGLE OUT THERE
from MONK

Words and Music by
RANDY NEWMAN

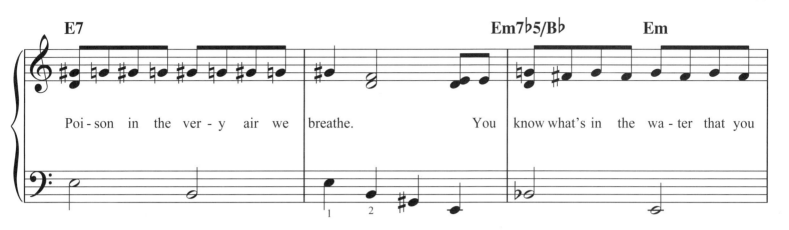

Poi - son in the ver - y air we breathe. You know what's in the wa - ter that you

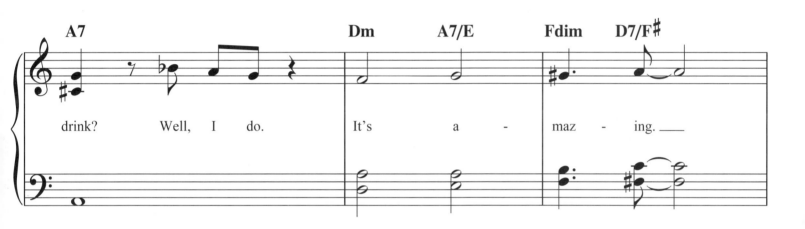

drink? Well, I do. It's a - maz - ing. ____

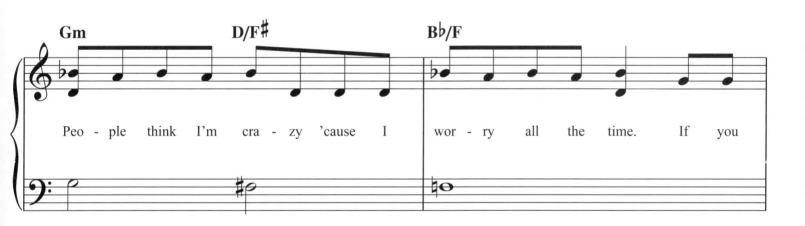

Peo - ple think I'm cra - zy 'cause I wor - ry all the time. If you

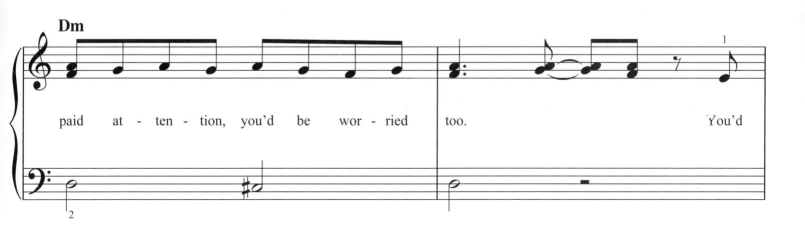

paid at - ten - tion, you'd be wor - ried too. You'd

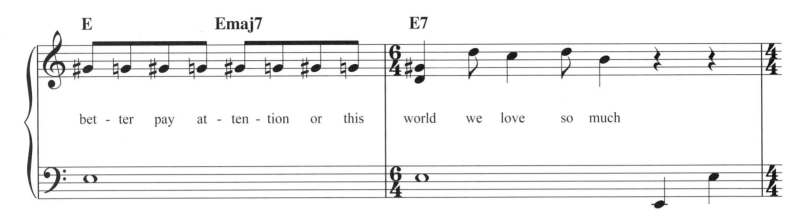

bet - ter pay at - ten - tion or this world we love so much

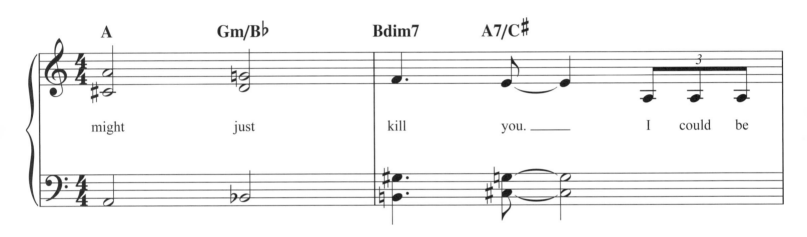

might just kill you. _____ I could be

wrong now. But I don't think so, 'cause it's a jun - gle out there.

It's a jun - gle out there.

LOVE BOAT THEME

from the Television Series

Words and Music by CHARLES FOX
and PAUL WILLIAMS

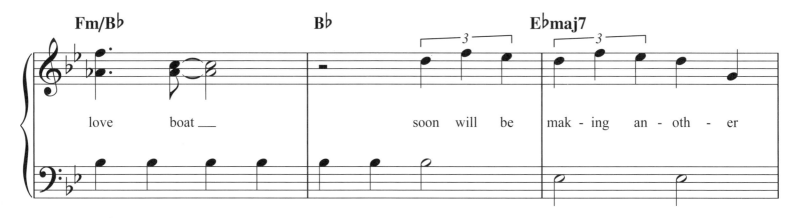

Fm/B♭   **B♭**   **E♭maj7**

love boat ___ soon will be mak - ing an - oth - er

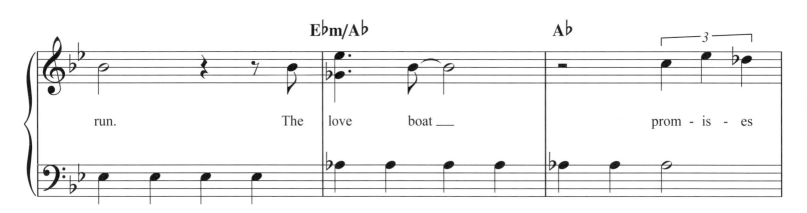

E♭m/A♭   **A♭**

run. The love boat ___ prom - is - es

D♭maj7   **C7sus**   **Fm**   **Fm(maj7)/E**

some - thing for ev - 'ry - one. Set a course for ad - ven - ture, your

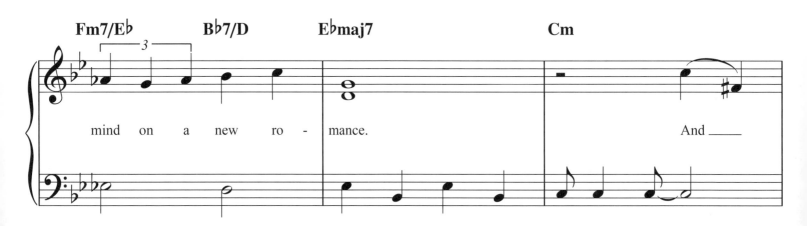

Fm7/E♭   **B♭7/D**   **E♭maj7**   **Cm**

mind on a new ro - mance. And ___

JEOPARDY THEME

Music by MERV GRIFFIN

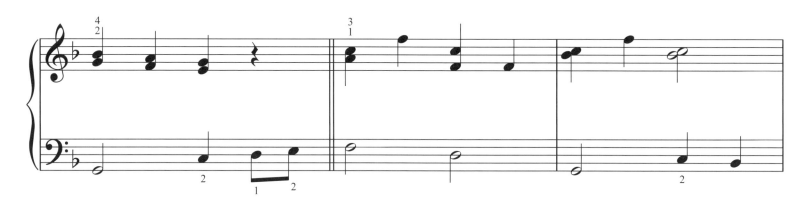

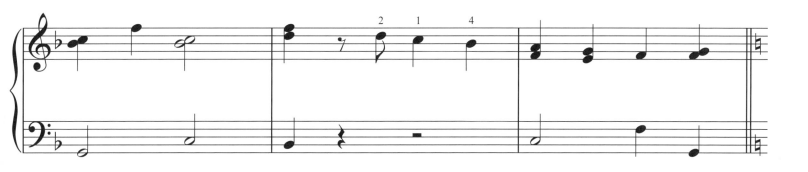

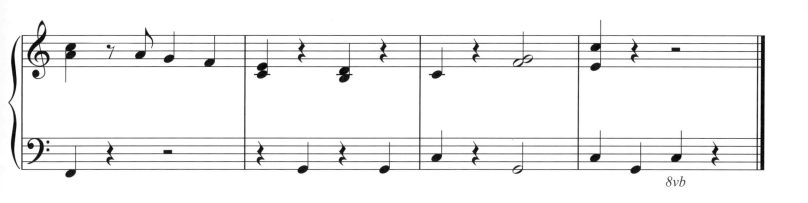

8vb

LAW AND ORDER

By MIKE POST

Moderate Rock

MICKEY MOUSE CLUBHOUSE THEME

Words and Music by JOHN LINNELL
and JOHN C. FLANSBURGH

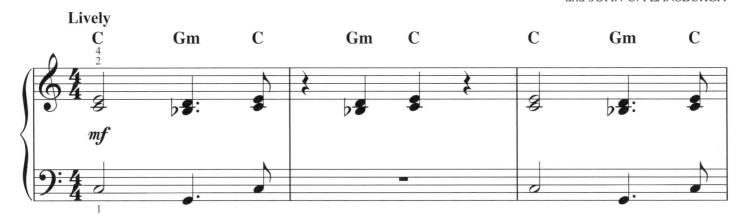

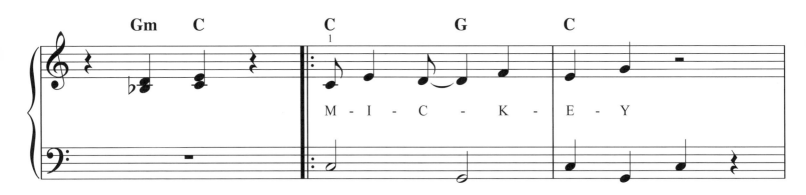

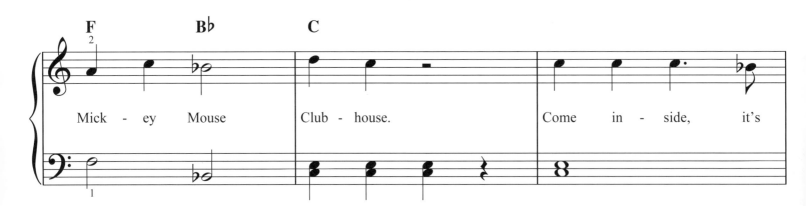

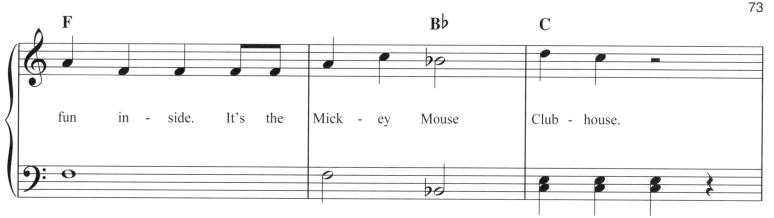

fun in - side. It's the Mick - ey Mouse Club - house.

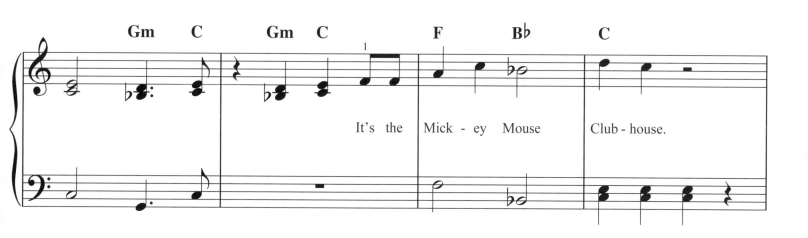

It's the Mick - ey Mouse Club - house.

Come in - side, it's fun in - side. M - I - C - K -

E - Y M - O - U - S - E.

MISSION: IMPOSSIBLE THEME

from the Paramount Television Series MISSION: IMPOSSIBLE

By LALO SCHIFRIN

Moderately, with a steady beat

THE MUPPET SHOW THEME
from the Television Series

Words and Music by JIM HENSON
and SAM POTTLE

Bright Ragtime

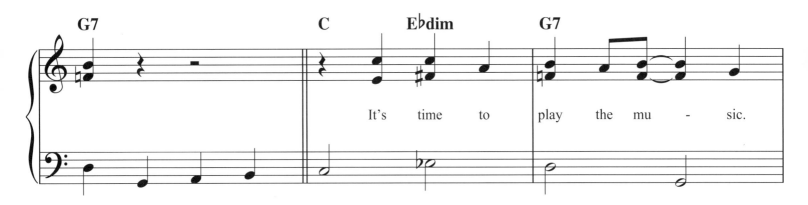

It's time to play the mu - sic.

It's time to light the lights. ___ It's time to

meet the Mup - pets on The Mup - pet Show ___ to - night.

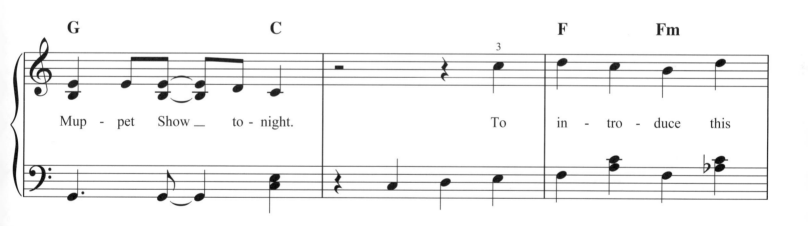

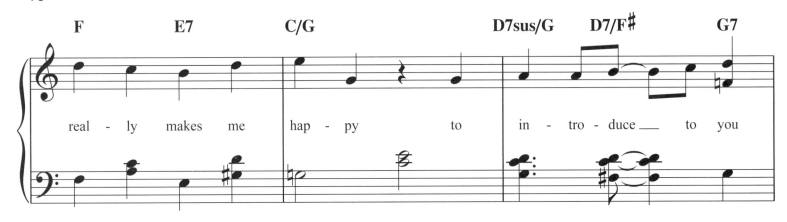

F   E7   C/G   D7sus/G   D7/F♯   G7

real - ly makes me | hap - py to | in - tro - duce ___ to you

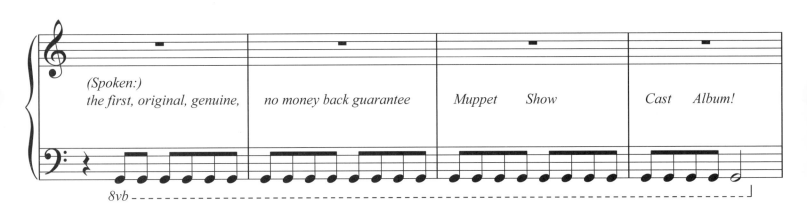

(Spoken:)
the first, original, genuine, | *no money back guarantee* | *Muppet   Show* | *Cast   Album!*

8vb ---

C   E♭dim   G7   C   E♭dim

(Sung:) It's time to | put on make - up. | It's time to

G7   C   C/B♭   F/A   Fm/A♭

dress up right. ___ | It's time to | get things start - ed on the

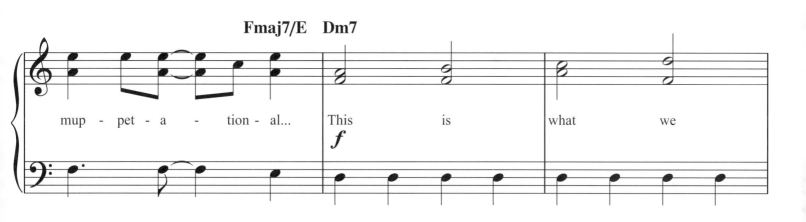

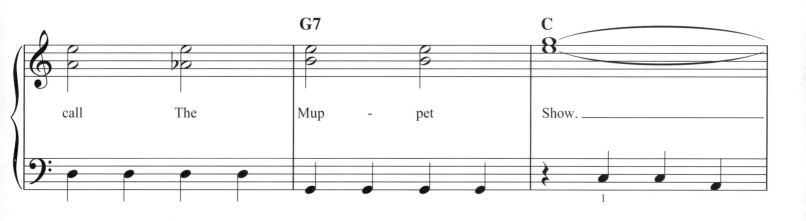

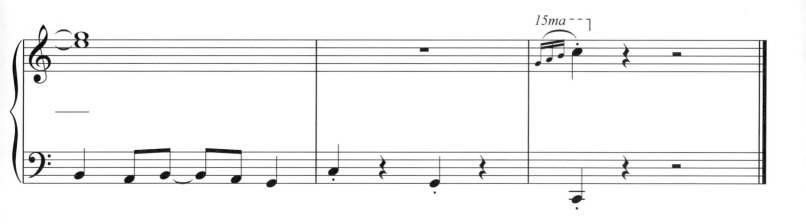

NADIA'S THEME
from THE YOUNG AND THE RESTLESS

By BARRY DeVORZON
and PERRY BOTKIN, JR.

Moderately, with expression

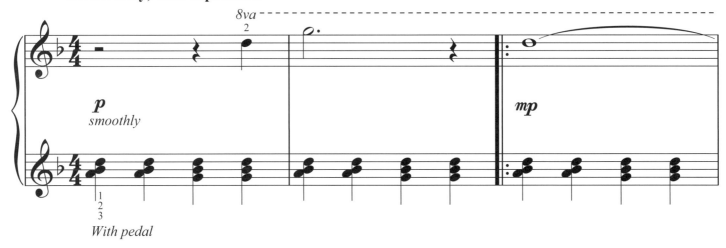

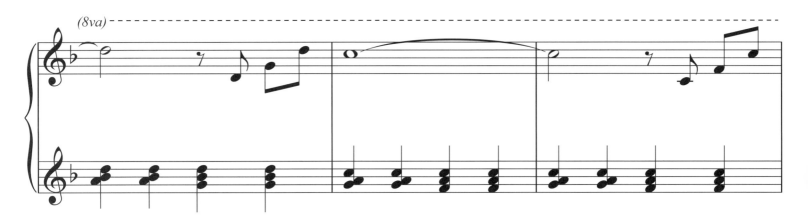

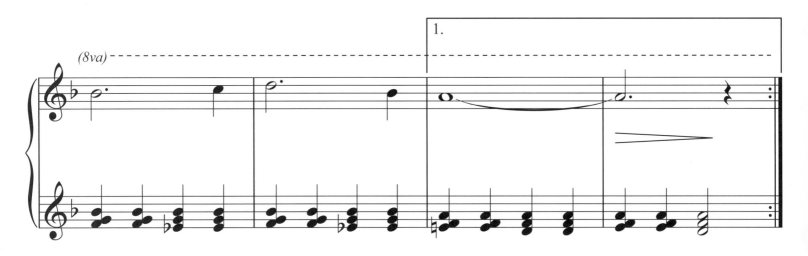

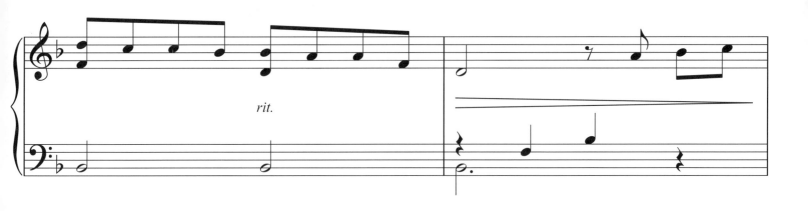

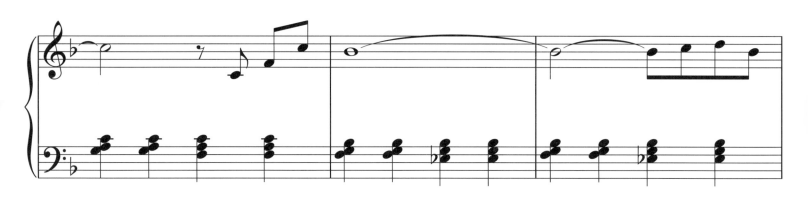

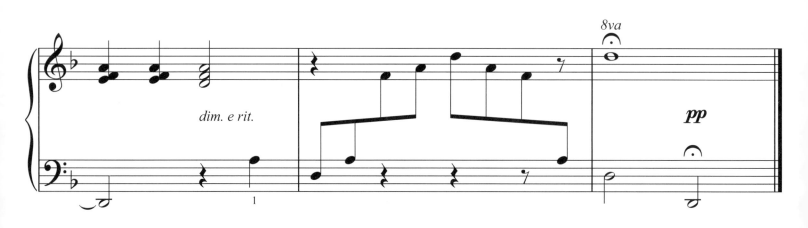

NFL ON FOX THEME

from the Fox Sports Broadcasts of THE NFL ON FOX

By PHIL GARROD,
REED HAYS and *SCOTT SCHREER*

March, in 2

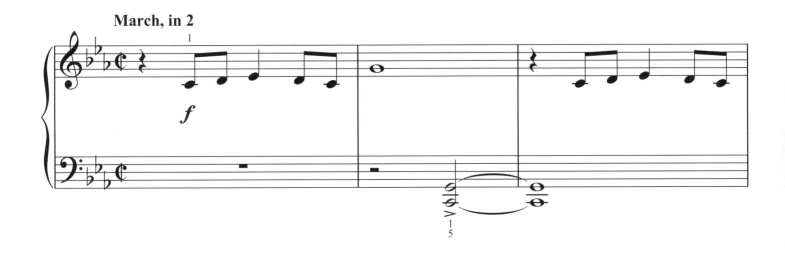

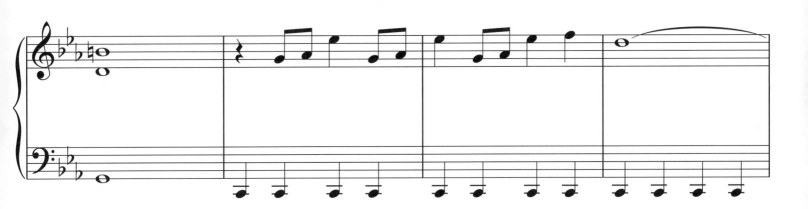

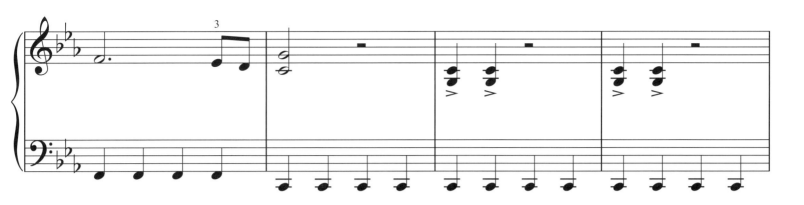

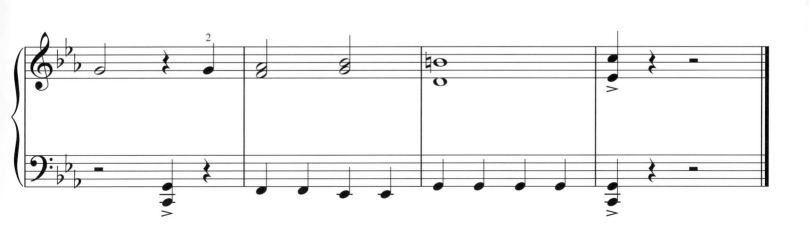

THE ODD COUPLE

Theme from the Paramount Television Series THE ODD COUPLE

Words by SAMMY CAHN
Music by NEAL HEFTI

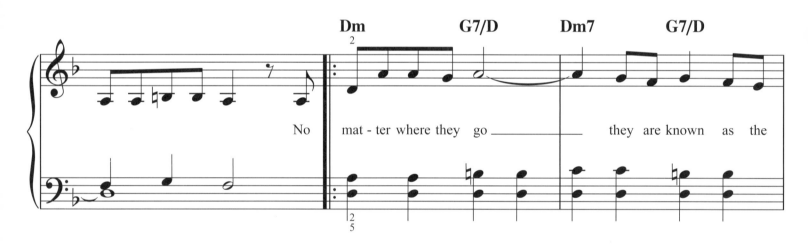

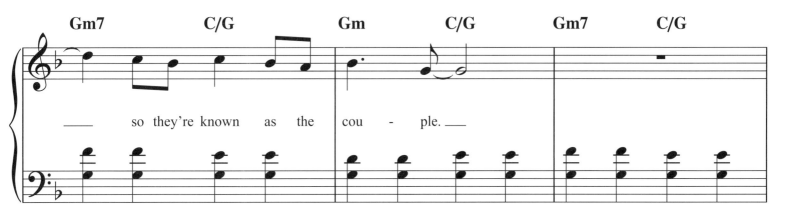

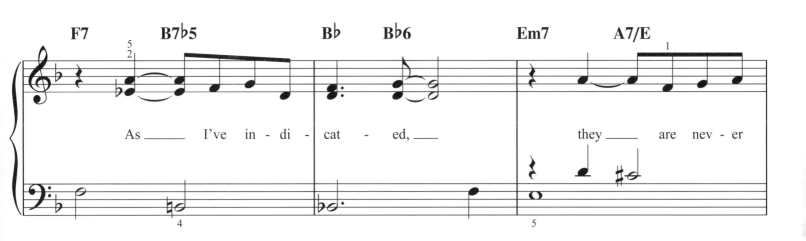

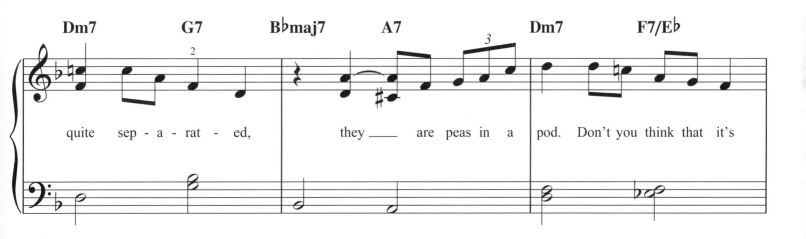

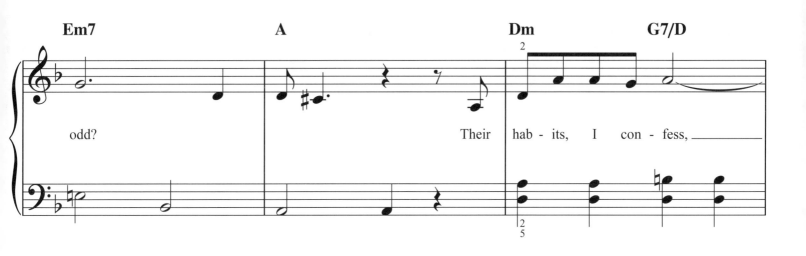

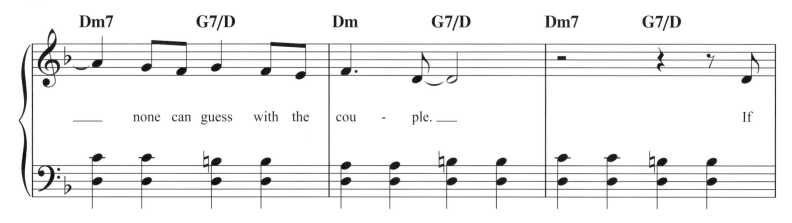

none can guess with the cou - ple.___ If

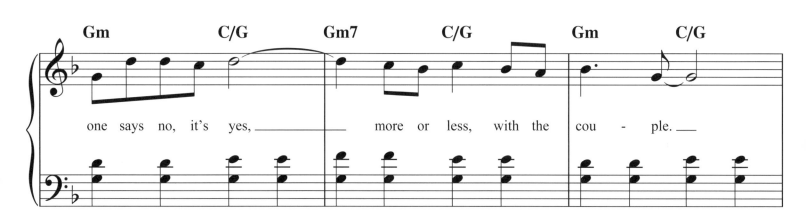

one says no, it's yes,_____ more or less, with the cou - ple.___

But ___ they're laugh - pro - vok - ing; ___

yet ___ they real - ly don't know they're jok - ing. Don't you find _____ when love is

THE OFFICE – THEME
from THE OFFICE

By JAY FERGUSON

PAW PATROL THEME

Words and Music by JEFF COHEN,
MOLLY KAYE, SCOTT KRIPPAYNE
and MICHAEL "SMIDI" SMITH

Moderately fast

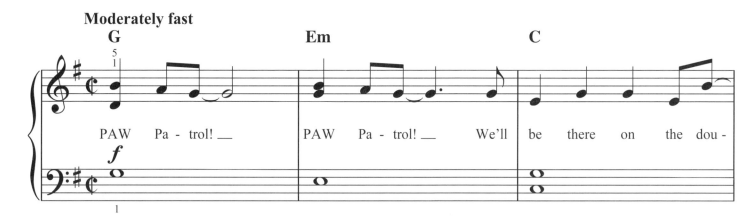

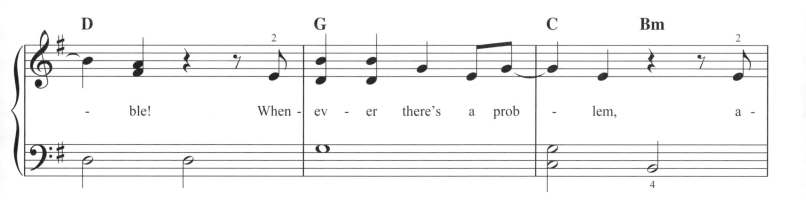

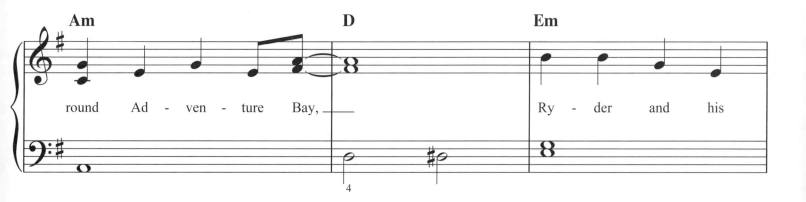

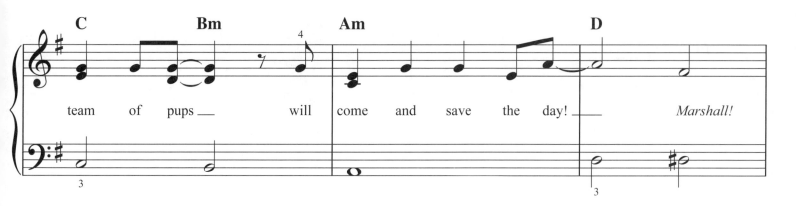

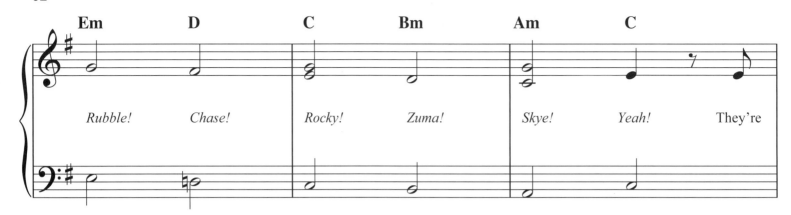

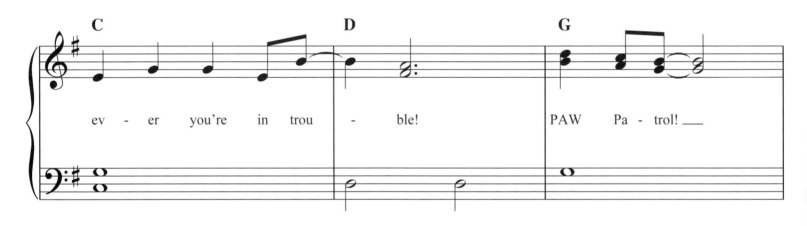

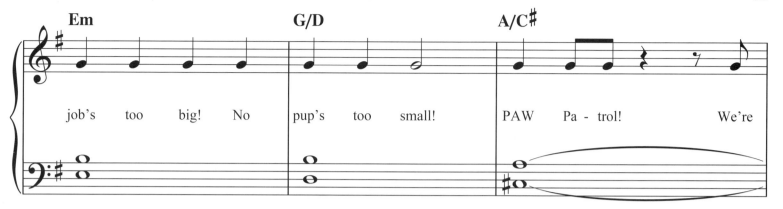

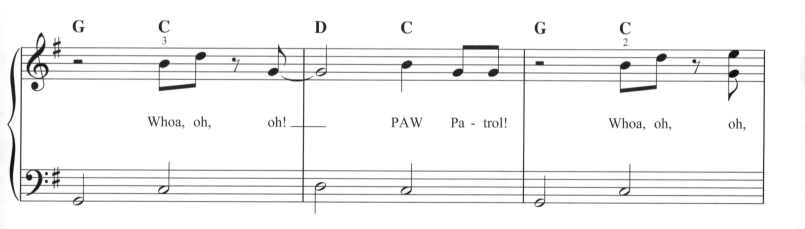

PARKS AND RECREATION THEME

Words and Music by GABY MORENO
and VINCENT JONES

Moderately fast

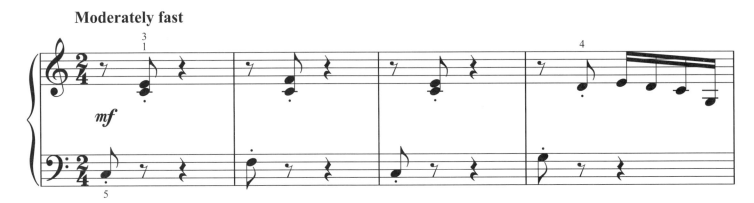

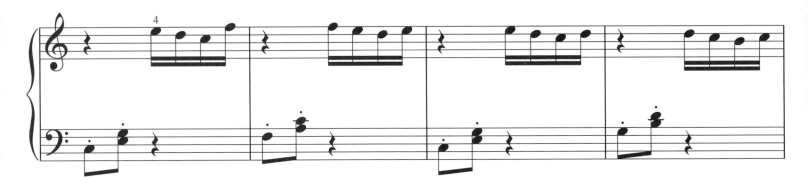

PRICE IS RIGHT – OPENING THEME

By EDWARD KALEHOFF

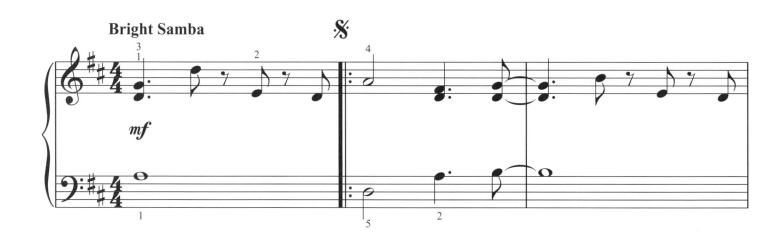

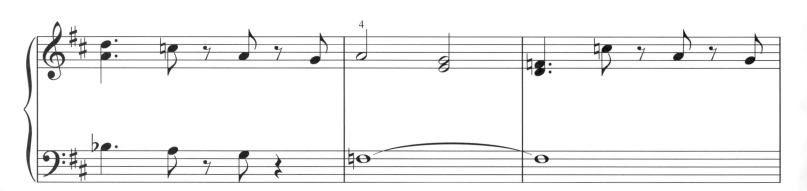

To Coda ⊕

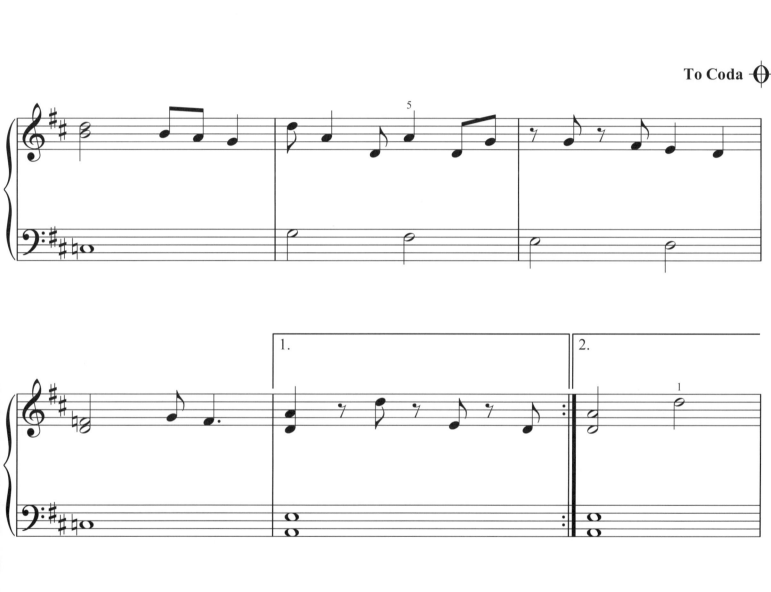

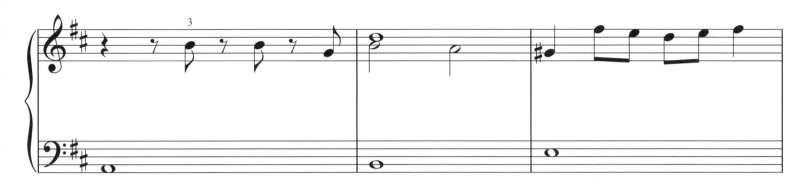

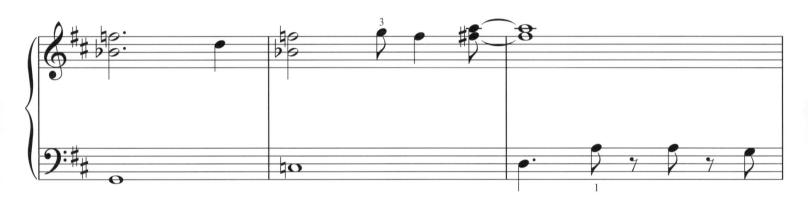

D.S. al Coda

CODA

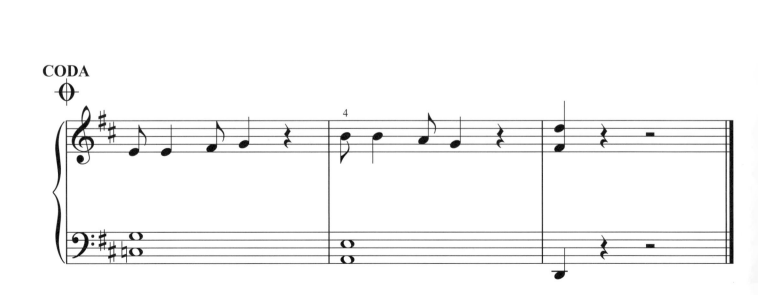

PERRY MASON THEME
from the Television Series

By FRED STEINER

Slow and dramatic

SAVED BY THE BELL

from the Television Series

Words and Music by
SCOTT GALE

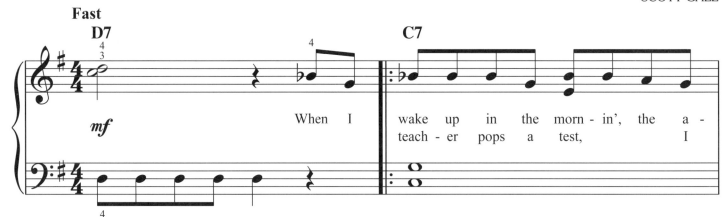

When I wake up in the morn-in', the a- /
teach-er pops a test, I

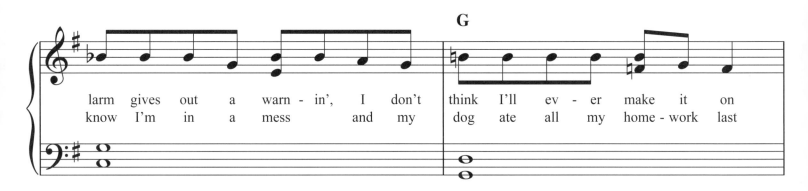

larm gives out a warn-in', I don't think I'll ev-er make it on /
know I'm in a mess and my dog ate all my home-work last

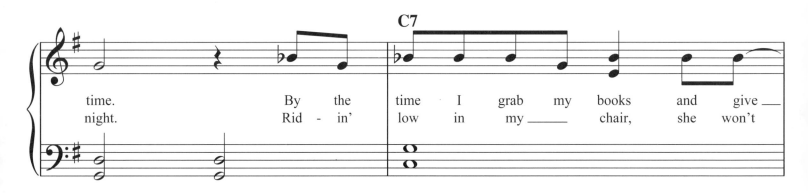

time. By the time I grab my books and give ___ /
night. Rid-in' low in my ___ chair, she won't

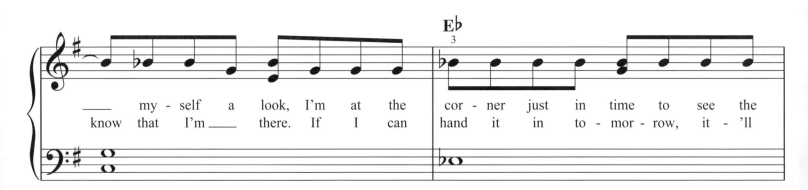

___ my-self a look, I'm at the cor-ner just in time to see the /
know that I'm ___ there. If I can hand it in to-mor-row, it -'ll

SESAME STREET THEME

from the Television Series SESAME STREET

Words by BRUCE HART,
JON STONE and JOE RAPOSO
Music by JOE RAPOSO

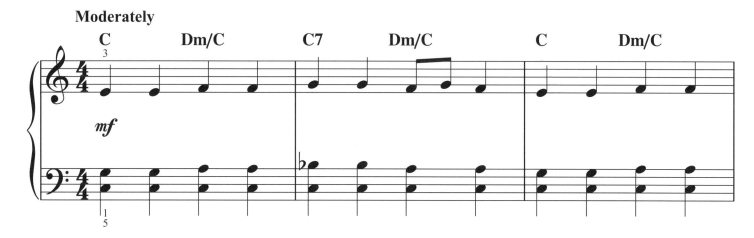

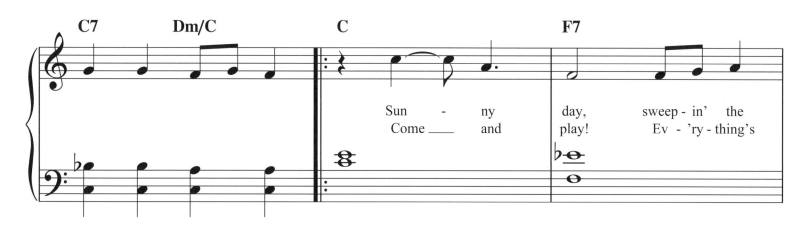

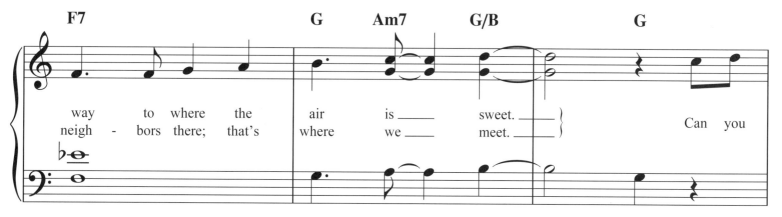

way   to   where   the   air   is ____   sweet. ____
neigh - bors there; that's   where   we ____   meet. ____   Can   you

tell   me   how   to   get,   how   to   get   to   Ses - a - me   Street? _

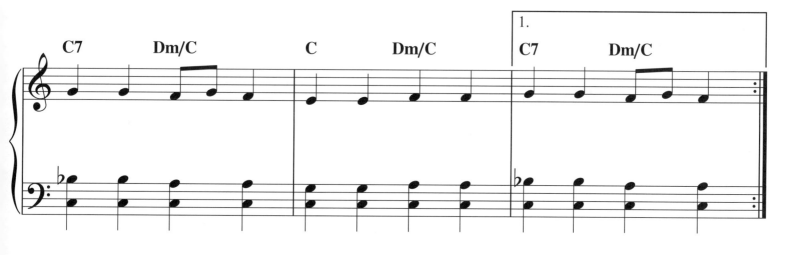

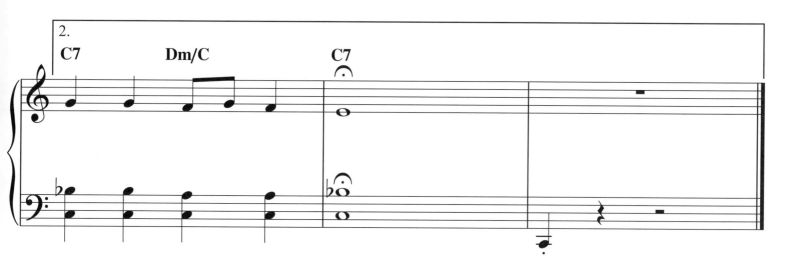

THEME FROM THE SIMPSONS™

from the Twentieth Century Fox Television Series THE SIMPSONS

Music by
DANNY ELFMAN

Moderately fast, in 2

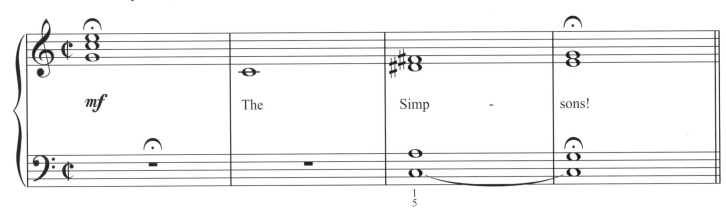

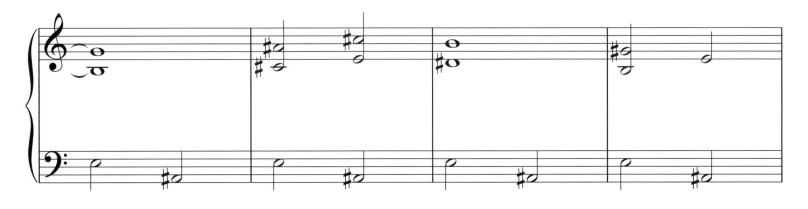

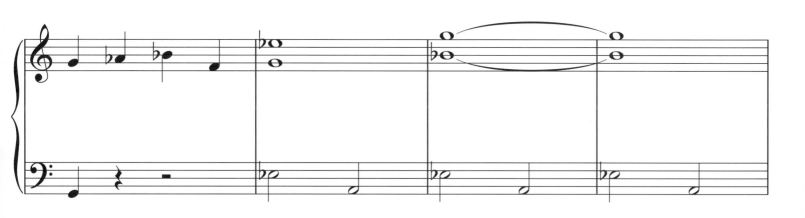

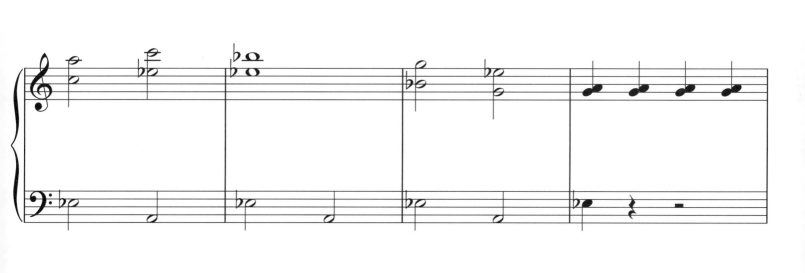

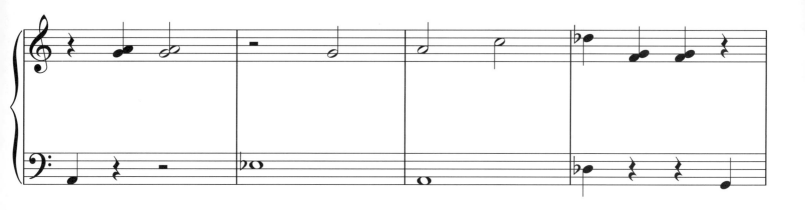

THEME FROM "STAR TREK®"

from the Paramount Television Series STAR TREK

Words by GENE RODDENBERRY
Music by ALEXANDER COURAGE

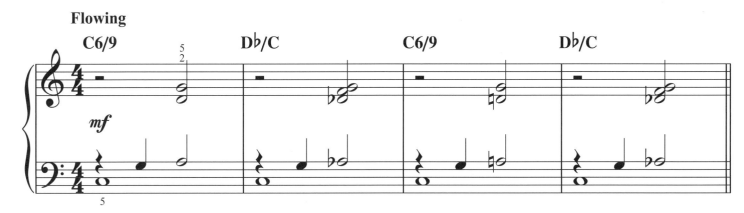

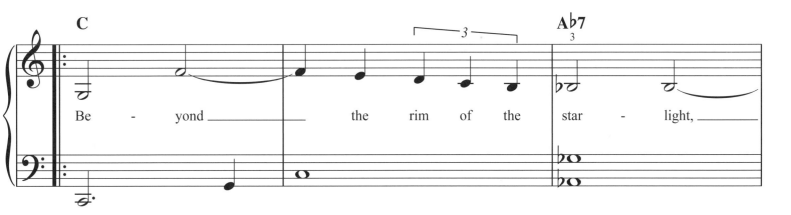

Be - yond ____ the rim of the star - light, ____

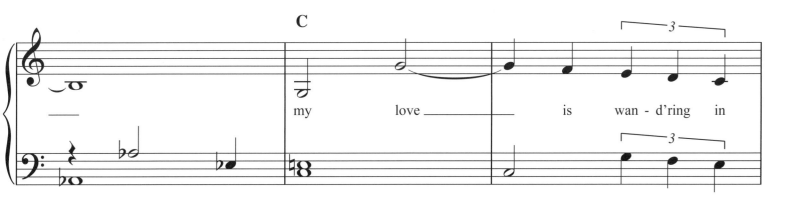

my love ____ is wan - d'ring in

star flight. ____ I know he'll

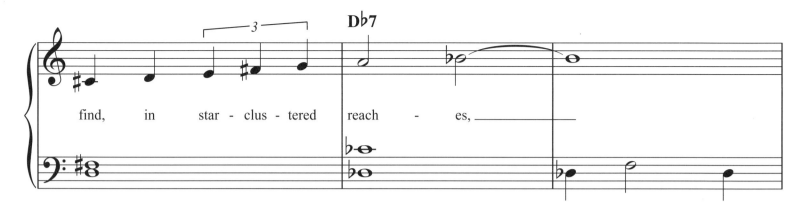

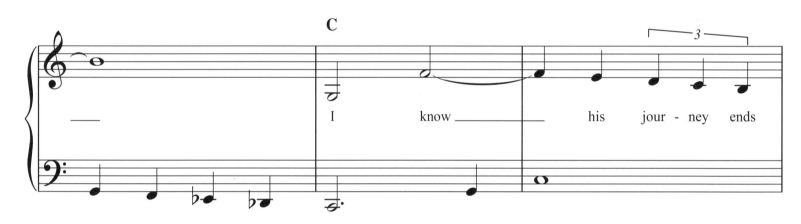

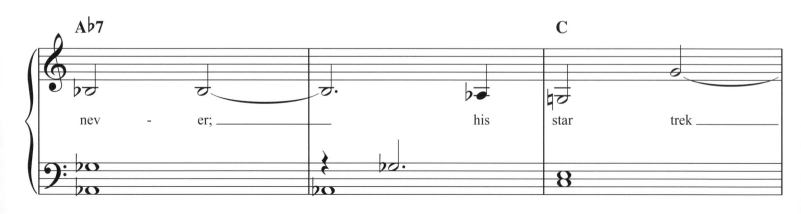

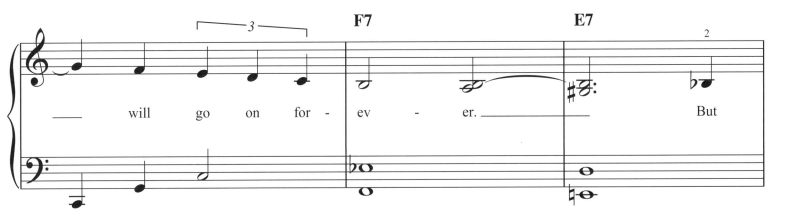

will go on for - ev - er. _____ But

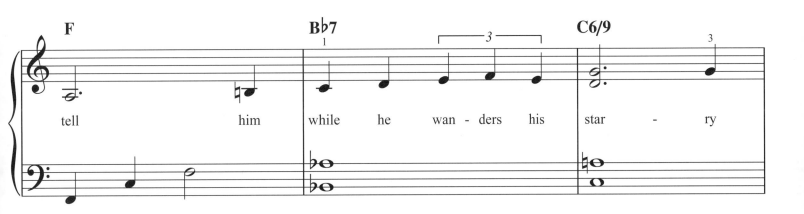

tell him while he wan - ders his star - ry

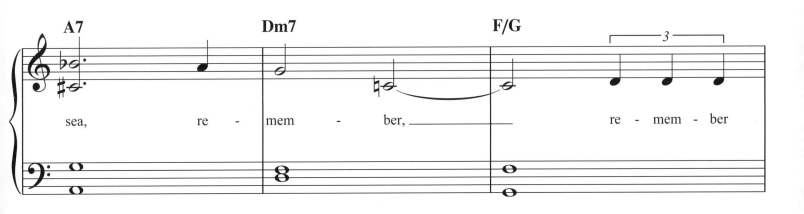

sea, re - mem - ber, _____ re - mem - ber

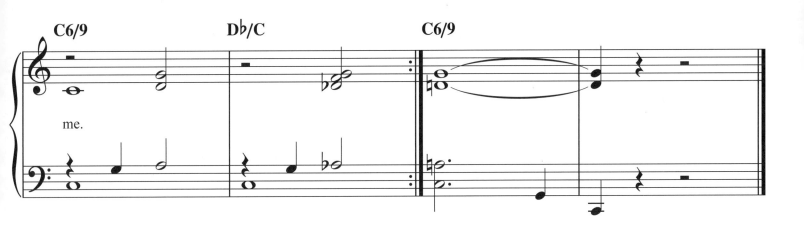

me.

THE SKYE BOAT SONG
Theme from the original series OUTLANDER

Traditional Music
Lyrics by ROBERT LOUIS STEVENSON
Arranged by BEAR McCREARY

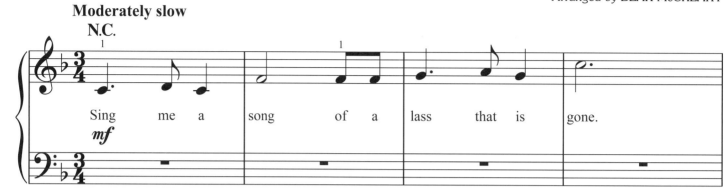

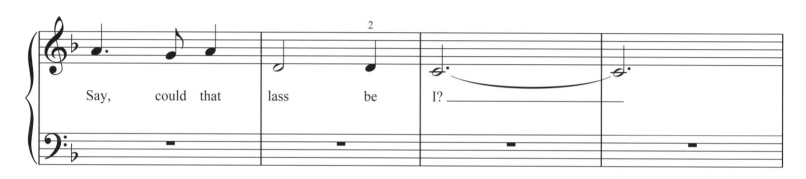

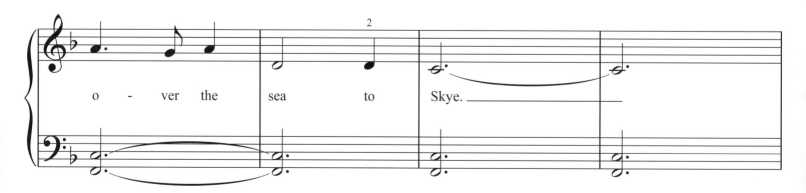

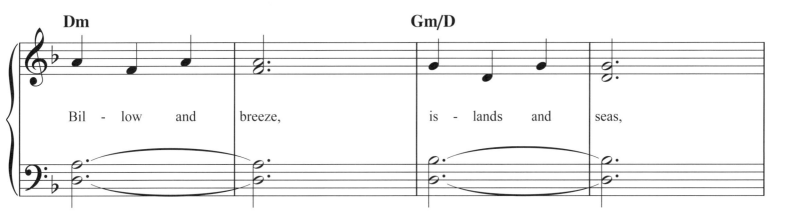

Dm   Gm/D

Bil - low and breeze,   is - lands and seas,

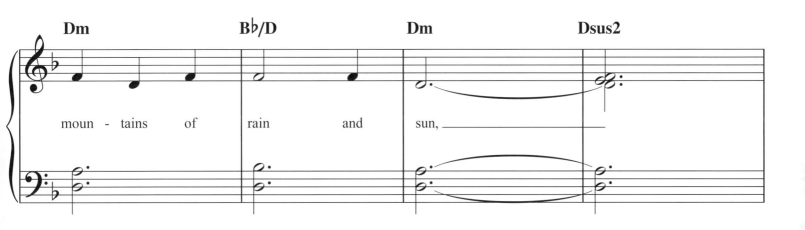

Dm   B♭/D   Dm   Dsus2

moun - tains of rain and sun, _____

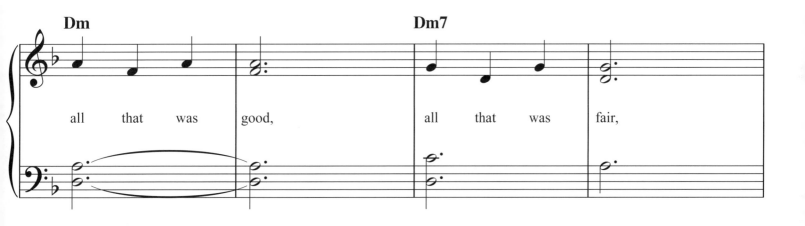

Dm   Dm7

all that was good,   all that was fair,

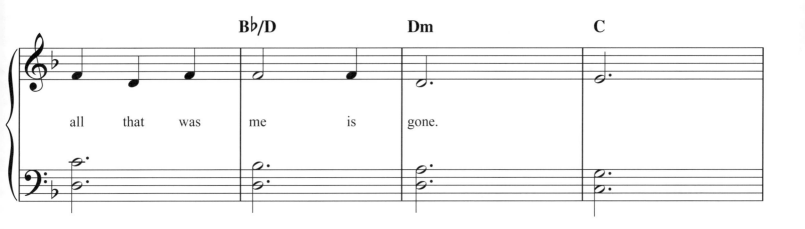

B♭/D   Dm   C

all that was me is gone.

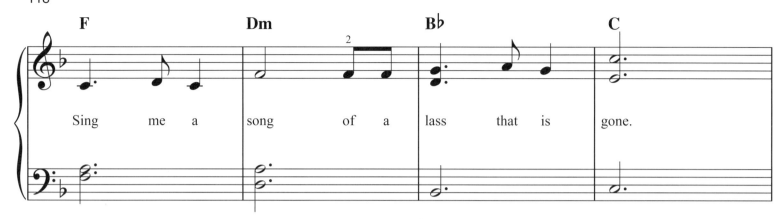

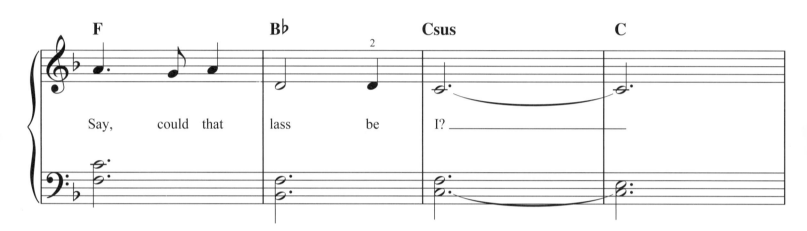

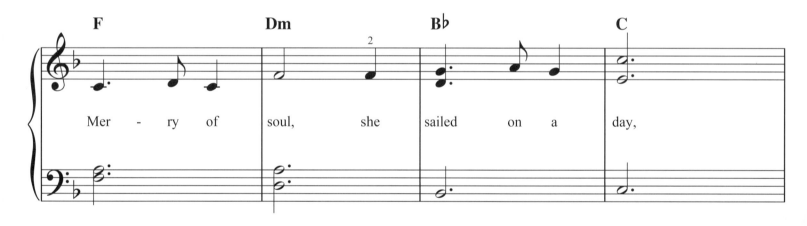

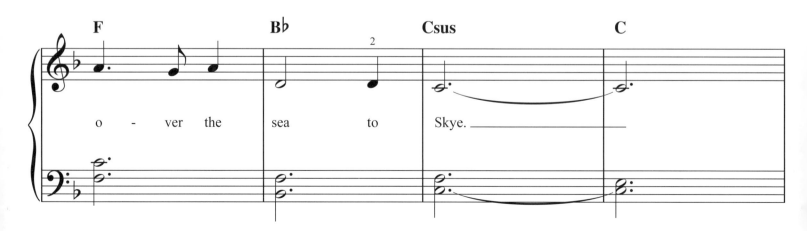

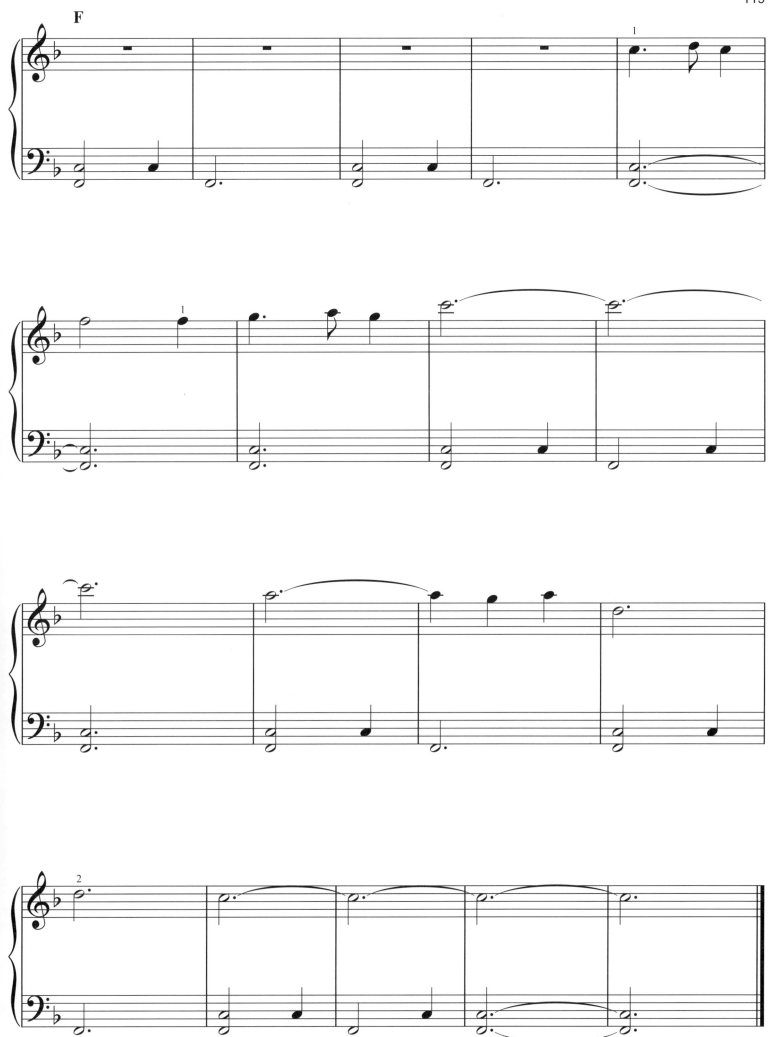

SOUTH PARK THEME

from the TV series SOUTH PARK

Words and Music by BRIAN KEI MANTIA,
LESLIE E. CLAYPOOL and REID LALONDE

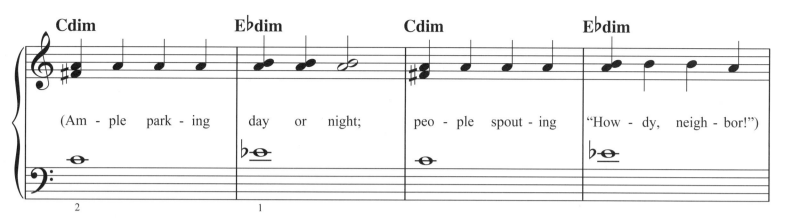

SPONGEBOB SQUAREPANTS THEME SONG

from SPONGEBOB SQUAREPANTS

Words and Music by MARK HARRISON,
BLAISE SMITH, STEVE HILLENBURG
and DEREK DRYMON

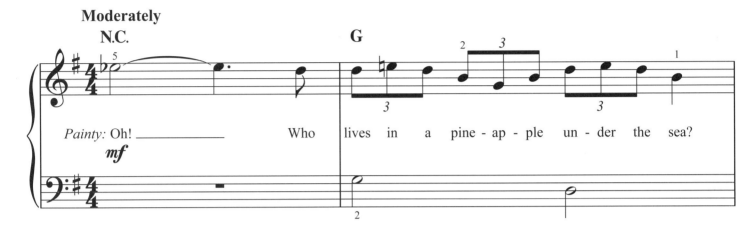

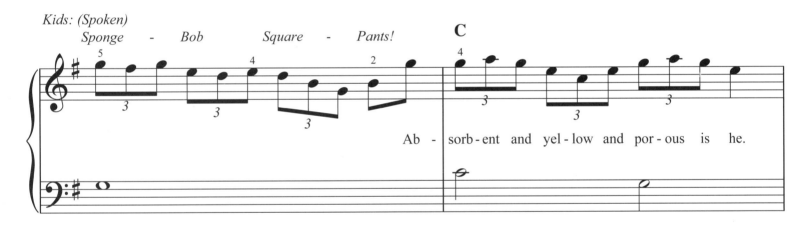

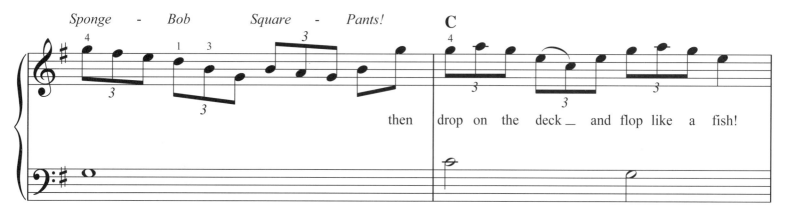

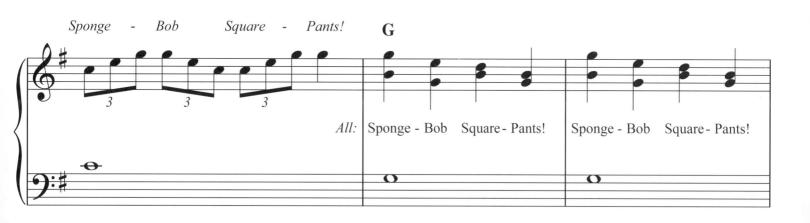

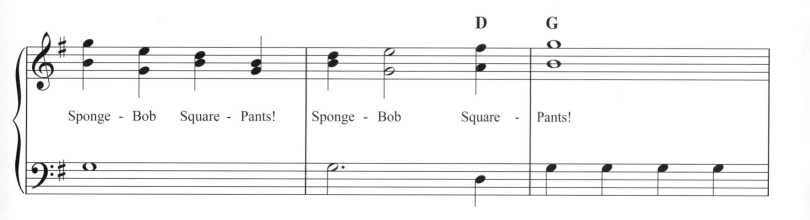

SONG FROM M*A*S*H
(Suicide Is Painless)
from M*A*S*H

Words and Music by MIKE ALTMAN
and JOHNNY MANDEL

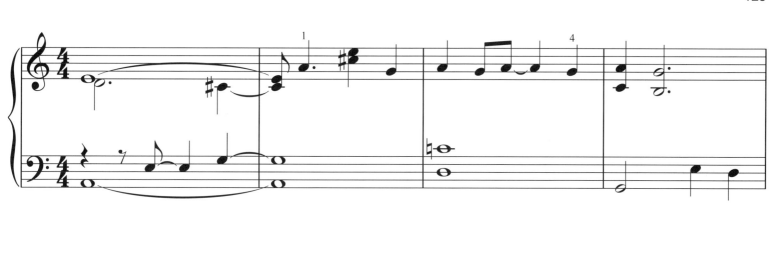

THE WALKING DEAD – MAIN TITLE

from THE WALKING DEAD

By BEAR McCREARY
and STEVEN KAPLAN

Moderately fast, in 2

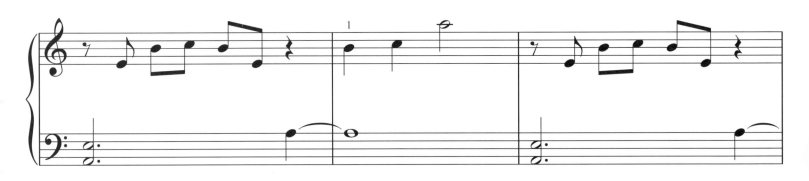

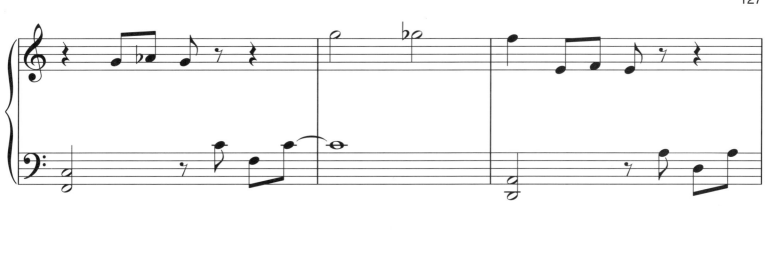

WHERE EVERYBODY KNOWS YOUR NAME

Theme from the Paramount Television Series CHEERS

Words and Music by GARY PORTNOY
and JUDY HART ANGELO

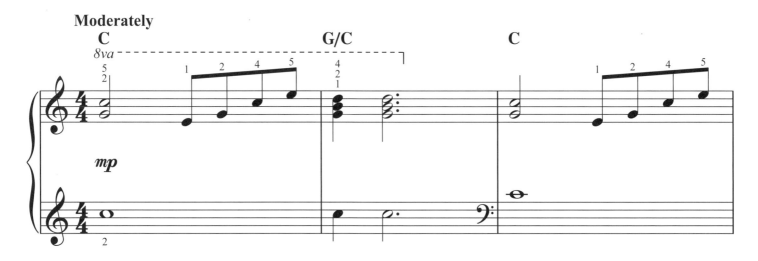

Mak-ing your way ___ in the world to-day ___ takes
Climb-ing the walls ___ when no one calls; ___ you've

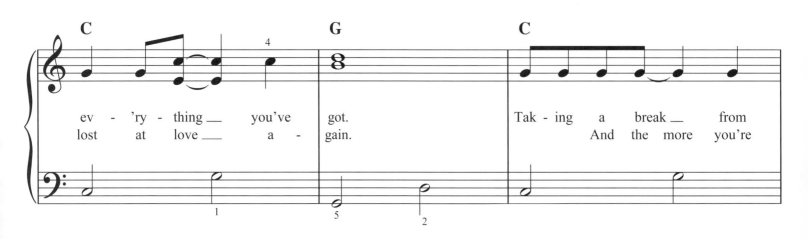

ev-'ry-thing ___ you've got. Tak-ing a break ___ from
lost at love ___ a- gain. And the more you're

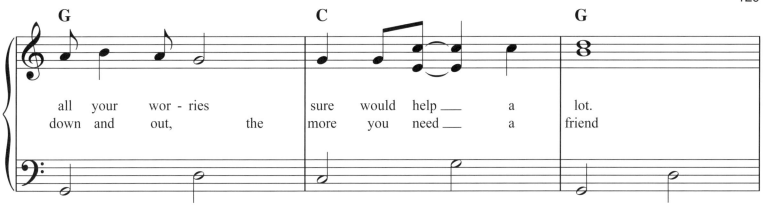

all your wor - ries | the sure would help ___ a | lot.
down and out, | the more you need ___ a | friend

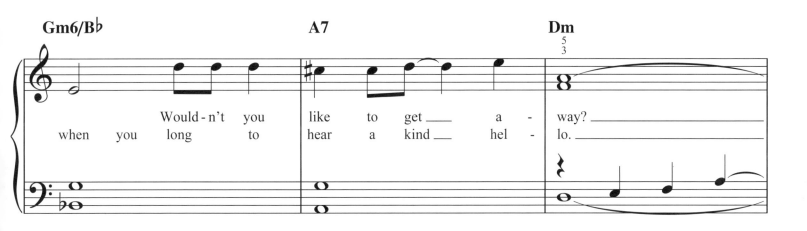

Would - n't you | like to get ___ a - | way? ___
when you long to | hear a kind ___ hel - | lo. ___

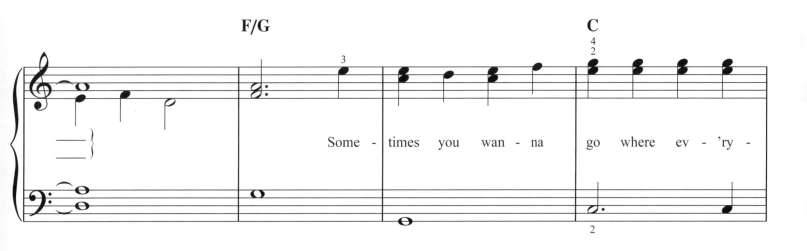

Some - times you wan - na | go where ev - 'ry -

bod - y knows ___ your | name, ___ | | and they're

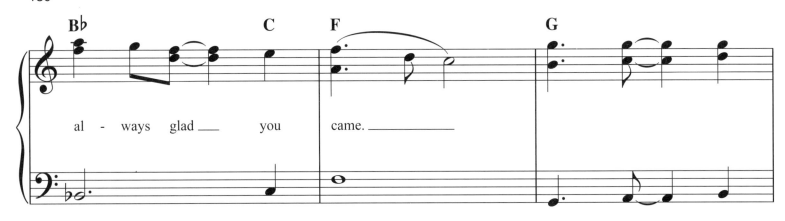

al - ways glad ___ you came. ___

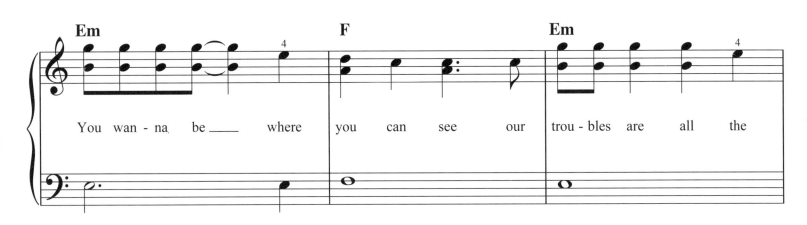

You wan - na be ___ where you can see our trou - bles are all the

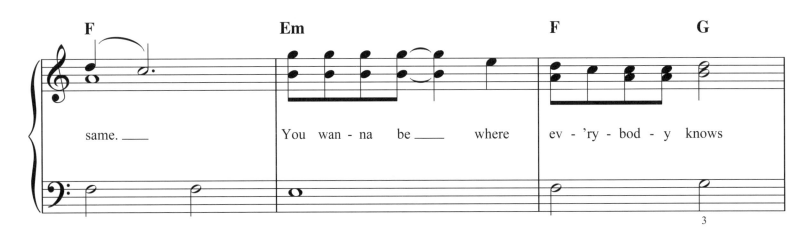

same. ___ You wan - na be ___ where ev - 'ry - bod - y knows

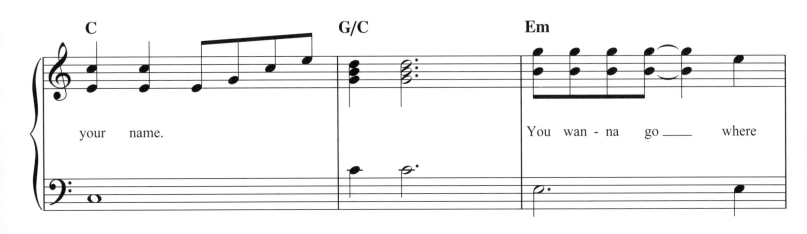

your name. You wan - na go ___ where

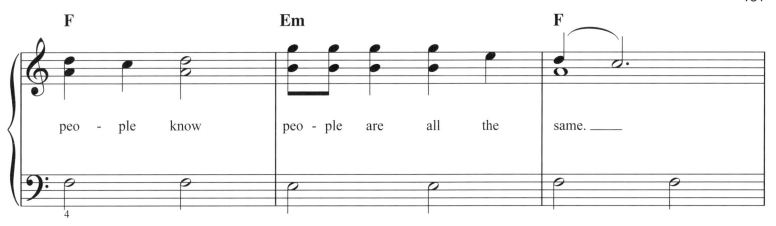

peo - ple know peo - ple are all the same. ___

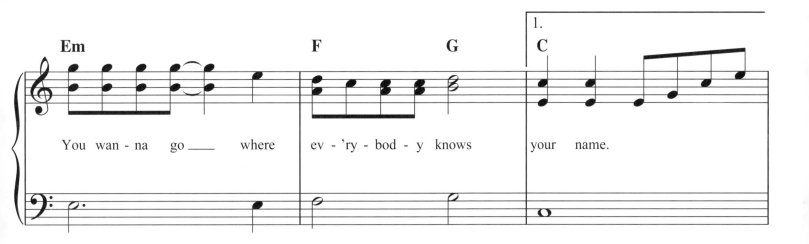

You wan - na go ___ where ev - 'ry - bod - y knows your name.

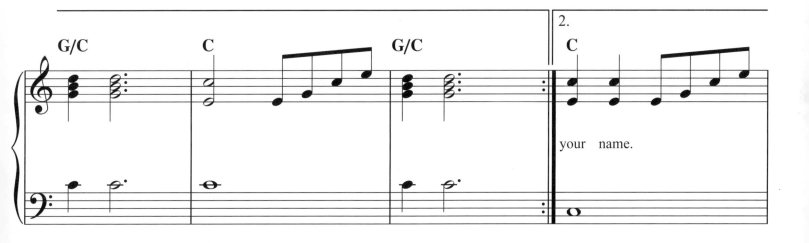

your name.

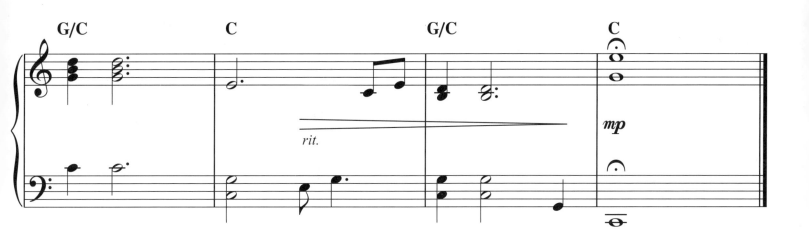

WON'T YOU BE MY NEIGHBOR?
(It's a Beautiful Day in the Neighborhood)
from MISTER ROGERS' NEIGHBORHOOD

Words and Music by
FRED ROGERS

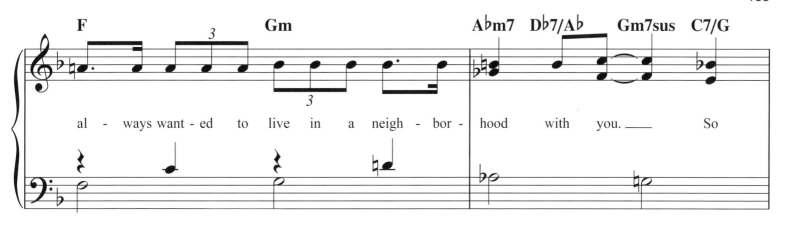

al - ways want-ed to live in a neigh - bor - hood with you.___ So

let's make the most of this beau - ti - ful day, since we're to - geth - er we might as well say,

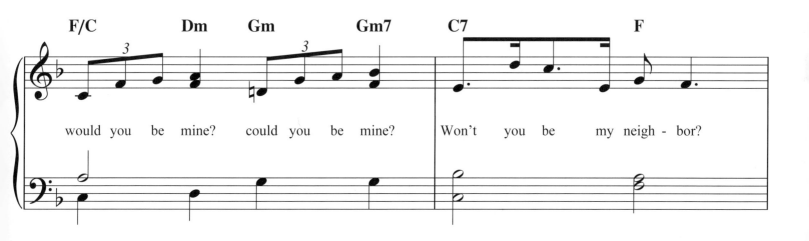

would you be mine? could you be mine? Won't you be my neigh - bor?

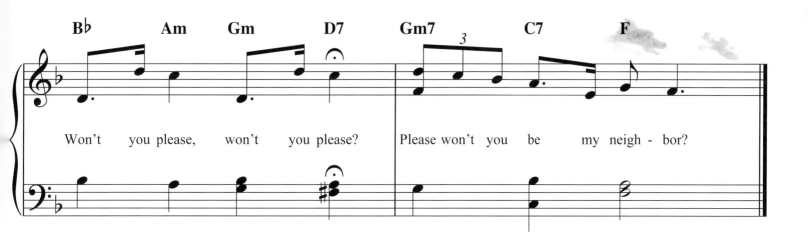

Won't you please, won't you please? Please won't you be my neigh - bor?

THEME FROM THE X-FILES

from the Twentieth Century Fox Television Series THE X-FILES

By MARK SNOW

THE WEST WING
(Main Title)

By W.G. SNUFFY WALDEN